English for Mass Communication

— 2020 Edition —

Hirofumi Horie
Kaori Kato
Kazuhisa Konishi
Shuji Miyazaki
Yasuko Uchino

ASAHI PRESS

音声再生アプリ「リスニング・トレーナー」を使った 音声ダウンロード

朝日出版社開発のアプリ、「リスニング・トレーナー（リストレ）」を使えば、教科書の音声を
スマホ、タブレットに簡単にダウンロードできます。どうぞご活用ください。

◉ アプリ【リスニング・トレーナー】の使い方

《アプリのダウンロード》

App Store または Google Play から
「リスニング・トレーナー」のアプリ
（無料）をダウンロード

App Storeは
こちら▶

Google Playは
こちら▶

《アプリの使い方》

① アプリを開き「コンテンツを追加」をタップ
② 画面上部に【15656】を入力しDoneをタップ

音声ストリーミング配信 》》》

この教科書の音声は、
右記ウェブサイトにて
無料で配信しています。

https://text.asahipress.com/free/english/

記事提供：CNN / The Japan Times / NIKKEI ASIAN REVIEW / Reuters / The Economist /
VOA News / The Wall Street Journal / 朝日新聞社 / 共同通信社 / AP / AFP / 毎日新聞社

写真提供：AP / CNN / iStock /KRT / The New York Times / アフロ / ロイター / AFP / WAA

表紙デザイン：大下賢一郎
本文イラスト：駿高泰子

English for Mass Communication — 2020 Edition —

は　し　が　き

　この本は、新聞・放送の英語ニュースをできるだけ多角的に学べるように編集したものです。

　時事英語を学ぶという行為は、「時事英語を理解すること」と「時事的な事柄や問題に関して英語でコミュニケーションを行うこと」の二つを学ぶことです。英語を読んだり、聞いたりすることは前者であり、時事的な事柄や問題に関して英語で書いたり、話したりすることが後者です。学習の順序としては、いうまでもなく、「理解」から入っていかなければなりません。英字新聞を読めず、英語放送を聞いてもよくわからない人が満足な英語を書けるはずがありませんし、話すことも期待できません。

　従って、この本の編集上の重点は、当然、「理解力の向上」に置かれています。この本では、政治・経済・外交・軍事・環境からスポーツにいたるまで多方面の英語ニュースを理解していただくように編集してあります。この教科書には授業の組み立て方に沿って色々な使い方があると思います。例えば、最もオーソドックスな使い方としては、まず時事英語の「理解力向上」に向けて二段階のアプローチをとることが可能です。まず第一段階として、英語ニュースを時事日本語に移しかえる能力を養うことです。そして第二段階でニュースの基本用語と英語ニュースの語学的特質を理解することです。従って、本書では各章において、まず、英語ニュースの読解と翻訳を行う構成となっています。そして、EXERCISE は、基本語学力を向上させることをねらいとしていますが、できるだけ「生きた英語」にアプローチしてもらうよう編集してあります。THE WORLD OF ENGLISH JOURNALISM は、主としてニュース英語の世界やニュース英語の語学的特質の理解を深めていただくために設けられています。また VOCABULARY BUILDUP は語彙力の充実をはかることをねらいとしています。この他にもいくつかの使い方があると思います。それぞれの授業の目標に即して最適な方法でお使い頂ければと思います。

　なお、本書における英語の綴りや句読点は、原則として、オリジナル記事の綴りに準拠しました。米国式・英国式で綴り方に違いがある場合も原文記事のままとし、必要に応じ注を加えてあります。例えば、「アメリカ合衆国」の略称は、米国式では U.S. となり、英国式では US となりますが、原文のままとしています。また、ニュース記事の冒頭における発信地の明示についても、内外のニュースを問わずオリジナル記事に準拠しました。

　本書の内容を一層充実させるため、読者諸氏のご教示を頂ければ幸いです。

　最後に、本書の出版にあたり種々のお骨折りを頂いた朝日出版社の日比野忠氏、加藤愛理氏、関麻央里氏、田所メアリー氏にこの場を借りて厚く御礼申し上げます。

編　著　者

CONTENTS

English for Mass Communication

NEWS 1

Japan's pro-constitution reform forces fall short of 2/3 upper house majority

Disk 1
(2)

Japanese Prime Minister Shinzo Abe's ruling bloc won a solid majority in an upper house election on Sunday but his coalition and allies fell short of a two-thirds majority needed to begin revising the pacifist constitution, public broadcaster NHK said.

Abe, who took office in December 2012 pledging to restart the economy and 5 bolster defence, is on track to become Japan's longest-serving premier if he stays in office until November, a stunning comeback after he abruptly ended a first, troubled one-year term in 2007.

However, voter turnout fell below 50 percent for the first time in a national election since 1995, a sign many voters feel they lack an attractive option. 10

Abe's Liberal Democratic Party (LDP) and its junior partner, the Komeito Party, were assured 71 of the 124 seats being contested in parliament's 245-seat upper house, NHK showed.

(3)

However, NHK said the ruling bloc and its allies fell short of the 85 seats needed to retain the two-thirds "super majority" required to begin revising the constitution's 15 pacifist Article 9 to further legitimise the military, a controversial step.

Abe said the size of the victory showed voters wanted to debate changing the charter for what would be the first time since its enactment after Japan's defeat in World War Ⅱ.

"Of course, we cannot take the timing as a given, but I would like to achieve it 20 (constitutional reform) somehow during my term," Abe said on television on Sunday evening. His term as LDP president runs until September 2021.

Without the two-thirds majority, Abe is likely to try to lure other opposition lawmakers to back his proposal to enshrine the military in the constitution, but that could be tough with a lower house election certain between now and 2021. 25

Surveys show voters are divided over changing the charter, with opponents worried doing so would increase the risk of Japan getting entangled in US-led conflicts.

Any change must be approved by two-thirds of both houses of parliament and a majority in a public referendum. The LDP-led bloc has a two-thirds majority in the 30 lower house.

— Based on a report on Reuters.com —

〈ニュース解説〉 2019年7月、参議院議員の通常選挙が行われ、同年10月からの消費税の10%への増税、年金制度の将来に対する不安などの問題はありながら、安倍首相率いる連立与党は、参議院での過半数を維持した。1人区での統一候補擁立などで挑んだ野党も決め手に欠いた状態だった。ただ、安倍首相が目標として掲げている憲法改正については、参議院での発議に必要とされる3分の2の多数には届かなかった。

(Notes)

◆ **Japan's pro-constitution reform forces fall short of 2/3 upper house majority** 「改憲勢力3分の2の多数に届かず　参院選」［"pro-constitution reform forces" は憲法改正賛成派、改憲勢力。"upper house" は参議院を指す。同院の正式英語名称は "House of Councillors" だが、二院制議会の上院に相当するため、英語ニュースでは、日本の事情に不案内な読者を想定し、"upper house" の表現が使われる。同様に後出の "lower house" は衆議院（House of Representatives）。英語ニュースの見出し "headline" は、本記事のように冒頭段落の "lead" を要約する場合や記事内容から新たに書き下ろす場合がある。即時性と簡潔さを尊び、過去の事象にも現在形を用いる、冠詞を省略する等、独特のスタイルがある。なお、P.13"THE WORLD OF ENGLISH JOURNALISM（The headline）" 参照のこと］

◆ (L. 1)　**Japanese Prime Minister Shinzo Abe's ruling bloc** 安倍晋三首相率いる与党陣営

◆ (L. 1)　**solid majority** 安定多数（一般的には全委員会の委員長を掌握できる議席数を確保すること）

◆ (L. 2)　**coalition and allies** 連立及びそれに協力的な勢力（具体的には自由民主党及び公明党の連立与党と憲法改正議論に前向きな日本維新の会等を指す）

◆ (L. 3)　**to begin revising the pacifist constitution** 平和憲法の改正を発議する（"pacifist" は「平和主義の」の意。「無抵抗主義」や「良心的兵役拒否」を表す場合もある。日本国憲法第96条は、同憲法の改正は衆参両議院の3分の2以上の賛成で発議し、国民投票の過半数の賛成によると規定されている。後出の "the charter" も憲法の意。英国通信社 "Reuters" 配信記事のため、"revising" は英国つづりとなっている。後出の "defence" や "legitimise" も同様に英国つづり）

◆ (L. 3)　**public broadcaster NHK** 公共放送の NHK［"Japan Broadcasting Corporation" と呼ばれることもある。NHK の存在根拠は放送法にあり、予算、事業計画等は国会承認を要するが、国営（state-owned）ではない］

◆ (L. 5-6)　**restart the economy and bolster defence** 経済再生と防衛（力）増強

◆ (L. 6)　**Japan's longest-serving premier if he stays in office until November** もし（2019年）11月まで務めれば、歴代で在任期間が最長となる首相（安倍首相は、2019年7月21日の本ニュースの時点で、桂太郎、佐藤栄作に次いで歴代3位。同年11月20日に在任2887日となり桂太郎と並ぶ。"premier" は、中国、フランス、ロシア等で首相を表す。英語ニュースでは "prime minister" の代替表現として使われる）

◆ (L. 7-8)　**first, troubled one-year term** 数々のトラブルに見舞われ、1年で終わった一期目

◆ (L. 9)　**voter turnout** 投票率

◆ (L. 11)　**Liberal Democratic Party (LDP)** 自由民主党

◆ (L. 11)　**junior partner, the Komeito Party** 連立少数党の公明党

◆ (L. 12-13)　**the 124 seats being contested in parliament's 245-seat upper house** 参議院245議席中の改選124議席（国会の正式英語名称は "the Diet" だが、英語ニュースでは読者の理解を考慮し、議会を意味する "parliament" が多用される）

◆ (L. 15)　**the two-thirds "super majority"** 3分の2の「圧倒的多数」

◆ (L. 15-16)　**the constitution's pacifist Article 9** 平和主義の憲法第九条

◆ (L. 16)　**to further legitimise the military** 日本の軍事力保持を憲法上合法化する

◆ (L. 18-19)　**enactment after Japan's defeat in World War Ⅱ** 第二次大戦の敗北後に制定された

◆ (L. 22)　**term as LDP president** 自民党総裁としての任期（党則改正で2期6年から3期9年に延長され、2021年9月までとなった）

◆ (L. 25)　**a lower house election certain between now and 2021** 2021年までに実施される衆院選（本ニュース時点の衆議院議員の任期は2021年10月。不定冠詞 "a" は「あり得べき」の意）

◆ (L. 27-18)　**getting entangled in US-led conflicts** 米国主導の紛争に巻き込まれる

◆ (L. 29-30)　**and a majority in a public referendum** 国民投票における過半数

1. 本文の内容と一致するものには T (True) を、一致しないものには F (False) を記せ。

(　　　) (1) Prime Minister Abe's ruling camp narrowly gained in the upper house the two-thirds majority needed to begin a constitutional reform.

(　　　) (2) Mr Abe would become the longest-serving Japanese prime minister in November 2019.

(　　　) (3) The number of voters in the upper house election exceeded 50 percent of eligible voters.

(　　　) (4) Prime Minister Abe indicated neither a concrete time limit for reforming the constitution nor his preference.

(　　　) (5) Mr Abe will probably recruit other opposition lawmakers who will support his proposal to authorise the constituional status of military.

(　　　) (6) The next lower house election will be held before the end of 2020.

(　　　) (7) Anti-constitution reform forces worry about the possibility of Japan's unintended involvement in US-led military conflict.

2. 次の英文を完成させるために、(a) ～ (d) から最も適切なものを 1 つ選べ。

To change any part of the Japanese constitution, the amendment should be approved by＿＿＿＿

(a) both the parliament and a people's referendum with a two-thirds majority.

(b) both the parliament and a people's referendum with a simple majority.

(c) the parliament with a simple majority but a people's referendum with a two-thirds majority.

(d) the parliament with a two-thirds majority but a people's referendum with a simple majority.

音声を聞き、下線部を補え。（2回録音されています。1回目はナチュラルスピード、2回目はスロースピードです。）

Natural 4
Slow 6

A newly energized Osaka Ishin no Kai (One Osaka) emerged Monday following strong victories in Sunday's (1)_____, the Osaka mayor's office, the prefectural assembly and an increase in municipal assembly seats just two shy of a majority.

With Osaka Ishin now firmly (2)_____, Liberal Democratic Party and Komeito officials, reeling from their losses, are wondering if Sunday's results will translate into losses for their own candidates in upper house elections set for July. 5

Natural 5
Slow 7

At the same time, Osaka Ishin officials made clear Sunday and Monday that they will increase (3)_____ Komeito, in 10 particular over the question of whether to merge Osaka's 24 wards into four semiautonomous zones and do away with the current structure of the city council. Osaka Ishin (4)_____ while Komeito, along with the LDP, have opposed it.

While Osaka Ishin (5)_____ in the 83-seat municipal 15 assembly, the party won 40 seats. LDP and Komeito assembly members are also aware that Ichiro Matsui, who heads Osaka Ishin is extremely close to Prime Minister Shinzo Abe and Chief Cabinet Secretary Yoshihide Suga.

— Based on a report on Japantimes.com —

〈ニュース解説〉　日本維新の会の地域政党である「大阪維新の会」の候補が大阪府知事及び大阪市長のダブル選挙を制した。それぞれの前任者が知事と市長を辞任し、入れ替わりで立候補する手法は、維新の会の創設者である橋下徹氏が現党首の松井一郎氏と行ったものと同じだ。同党は、大阪府と大阪の各市を再編し、特別区とその他の自治体からなる大阪都を作ること（大阪都構想）を公約。同構想への賛否を問う住民投票に僅差で敗れてから4年、リターンマッチを目指し再始動した。同党は憲法改正にも前向きで、安倍政権とも近く、政界再編の台風の目と言われている。

(Notes)

Osaka Ishin no Kai (One Osaka) 大阪維新の会（One Osaka）（日本維新の会の地域政党。"One Osaka" は「大阪をひとつに」にという「大阪都構想」のキャッチフレーズ）　**the Osaka mayor's office** 大阪市長職　**the prefectural assembly** 府議会　**municipal assembly seats** 市議会の議席　**two shy of a majorrity** 過半数に2議席足りない　**upper house elections set for July** 7月に予定されている参議院選挙（News 1 参照）　**to merge Osaka's 24 wards into four semiautonomous zones** 大阪市の24の区を4つの準自治権を有する特別区に統合させる（大阪都構想を指す）　**do away with the current structure of the city council** 現行の市議会の体制を廃止する　**Ichiro Matsui** 松井一郎　**Chief Cabinet Secretary Yoshihide Suga** 菅義偉内閣官房長官

■問A　空所 (a) ～ (n) にそれぞれ入るべき1語を下記の語群から選びその番号を記せ。

内閣府　　　　　　→　Cabinet (a)
防衛省　　　　　　→　Ministry of (b)
金融庁　　　　　　→　Financial Services (c)
法務省　　　　　　→　Ministry of (d)
総務省　　　　　　→　Ministry of Internal Affairs and (e)
財務省　　　　　　→　Ministry of (f)
外務省　　　　　　→　Ministry of Foreign (g)
環境省　　　　　　→　Ministry of the (h)
文部科学省　　　　→　Ministry of (i), Culture, Sports, Science and Technology
厚生労働省　　　　→　Ministry of (j), Labour, and Welfare
農林水産省　　　　→　Ministry of Agriculture, Forestry and (k)
経済産業省　　　　→　Ministry of Economy, (l) and Industry
国土交通省　　　　→　Ministry of Land, (m), Transport and Tourism
国家公安委員会　　→　National Public Safety (n)

1. Affairs	2. Agency	3. Commission
4. Communications	5. Defense	6. Education
7. Environment	8. Finance	9. Fisheries
10. Health	11. Infrastructure	12. Justice
13. Office	14. Trade	

■問B　(a) ～ (f) にそれぞれ対応する英語表現を下記の語群から選びその番号を記せ。

(a) 憲法　　(b) 国会　　(c) 総選挙　　(d) 与党　　(e) 野党　　(f) 連立

1. coalition	2. constitution	3. Diet
4. general election	5. opposition party	6. ruling party

■問C　空所 (a) ～ (j) にそれぞれ入るべき1語を下記の語群から選びその番号を記せ。

自由民主党　→ (a) Democratic Party　　　　立憲民主党　→ (b) Democratic Party of Japan
国民民主党　→ Democratic Party for the (c)　　公明党　→ (d) Party
日本共産党　→ Japanese (e) Party　　　　日本維新の会　→ Nippon (f) no Kai
小選挙区制　→ single-seat (g) system　　　比例代表制　→ proportional (h) system
衆議院　　　→ House of (i)　　　　　　　参議院　　　→ House of (j)

1. Communist	2. constituency	3. Constitutional	4. Councillors
5. Ishin	6. Komeito	7. Liberal	8. People
9. representation	10. Representatives		

THE WORLD OF ENGLISH JOURNALISM

News defined ― ニュースは記者が決める？

掲載するニュースを決めるのは編集局（記者）だが、ニュースの定義には、世の中に起こっているすべてがニュースだという考えもある。しかし他方で、そのような様々な出来事からニュースにする価値あり（newsworthy）と記者が判断して選んだものがニュースだという考えもある。記者たちの中には、"We determine the news!" と公言して、ニュースは記者が作るものだと考えている人たちも多い。また、ニュースを選ぶ基準として、"what people want to know" と "what people need to know" の間のバランスを取ることも大切である。

このトピックを英文で読んでみよう。

How do you determine whether a current idea, event or problem is news? How do you recognize it, separating swiftly the news and the non-news in what happens? How can you be sure that it will interest readers, listeners, or viewers?

To answer these questions, examine the elements common in all news. These may also be termed news values, appeals, factors, determinants, or criteria. Even if one is missing, the reporter may question whether the happening is news.

The five news elements are: (a) timeliness, (b) nearness, (c) size, (d) importance and (e) personal benefit.

NEWS 2

Disk 1

Japan is wasting its last chance to avoid a major economic blunder

Japan is fumbling what looks like its last chance to avoid an unnecessary and economically damaging sales-tax hike.

The country's ruling Liberal Democratic Party published its policy priorities for a July election to the upper house of Japan's legislature on Friday, including a fresh commitment to increase the tax to 10 percent from 8 percent in October. The general ⁵ government deficit ran to 4.2 percent of Japanese GDP last year.

The LDP's latest statement makes the prospect of a snap election in the lower house — which might delay the tax increase — more far-fetched. Over the weekend, Japan's Nikkei newspaper carried a report suggesting the government is unlikely to call a second vote. ₁₀

Since Prime Minister Shinzo Abe came to office in 2012, Japan has recorded its longest period of nominal growth since the country's asset bubble burst in the early 1990s. Gains in Japan's Topix stock index beat all large developed markets outside the U.S. over the same period. There is no pressing need to junk that promising record now. ₁₅

The last sales-tax rise in 2014 dented Japan's recovery. Now growth is weaker, the international environment more uncertain, and the likelihood that the Bank of Japan will soften the blow even lower.

Some international financial outfits, like the Organization for Economic Cooperation and Development, have encouraged Japan's act of fiscal self-sabotage. ₂₀ The OECD noted the consumption tax would have to be raised to between 20 percent-26 percent for the country to run a primary budget surplus, without adding that such an increase would tank the economy.

Former International Monetary Fund chief economist Olivier Blanchard and co-author Takeshi Tashiro took a more realistic view in a paper published by the Peterson ₂₅ Institute for International Economics last month, noting that Japan may have to run primary deficits — or even increase them — for years to come if it doesn't want to curtail already fragile growth rates. With borrowing costs close to zero, it can afford to do so.

The economic evidence on eliminating budget deficits is overwhelming: ₃₀ economic growth is the key. Few countries reduce deficits through fiscal austerity alone. Those that do — like Greece, where GDP is still almost a quarter below its pre-financial crisis peak — are no model to follow.

— Based on a report on WSJ.com —

〈ニュース解説〉　少子高齢化社会が急速に進む日本は、年金・医療・介護などの社会保障制度の維持に必要な安定的財源を求めて、1989 年（平成元年）4 月に 3% の消費税を導入した。税率は 1997 年 4 月に 5%、2014 年 4 月には 8% へと引き上げられ、2015 年 10 月に 10% とする予定であった。しかし、景気への悪影響を考慮して増税は 2 度延期され、2019 年 10 月の実施予定となった。同年 7 月の参議院選挙で与党の自民・公明両党が改選議席の過半数を獲得、公約に掲げた消費税 10% に対する国民の信任を得たとして予定通り増税が実施される見通しとなったが、本ニュースが報じるように、現在の経済情勢下での消費税増税には賛否がある。

(Notes)

- ◆ (L. 1)　**fumble**　しくじる、台無しにする、扱いを失敗する
- ◆ (L. 2)　**sales-tax hike**　消費税増税［consumption tax や value-added（付加価値税）なども使われる］
- ◆ (L. 3)　**ruling Liberal Democratic Party**　与党自由民主党
- ◆ (L. 3)　**policy priority**　優先政策、重点政策
- ◆ (L. 4)　**upper house**　参議院（House of Councillors）
- ◆ (L. 4)　**legislature**　議会
- ◆ (L. 5-6)　**general government deficit**　一般政府債務（中央政府、地方政府及び社会保障基金の債務残高）
- ◆ (L. 6)　**GDP**　国内総生産（gross domestic product の略）
- ◆ (L. 7)　**snap election**　解散総選挙［snap は「急な」の意。解散総選挙は総選挙を行うために衆議院を解散することで、解散により全衆議院議員は任期満了を待たずに議員としての地位を失う］
- ◆ (L. 8)　**far-fetched**　不自然な、ありそうにない
- ◆ (L. 9)　**Nikkei newspaper**　日本経済新聞
- ◆ (L. 10)　**second vote**　（ここでは解散総選挙を指している。参議院選挙を 1 つ目の選挙（first vote）とすると、それに合わせて衆議院を解散して衆参同日選挙を実施するとの噂があったことから、衆議院選挙を second vote としている。実際には衆議院解散はなかった）
- ◆ (L. 11)　**come to office**　政権に就く
- ◆ (L. 12)　**nominal growth**　名目 GDP 成長（率）［物価変動調節前の名目ベースでの国内総生産の成長（率）］
- ◆ (L. 12)　**the country's asset bubble**　日本の資産バブル（1986 年 12 月〜 1991 年 2 月に起きた資産価格の急上昇を伴ったバブル経済）
- ◆ (L. 13)　**Topix**　東証株価指数［Tokyo stock price index、Topix（トピックス）。東京証券取引所第一部上場株式全銘柄を対象とする株価指数で「日経平均株価」とともに日本株の代表的な指標］
- ◆ (L. 14)　**junk**　捨てる
- ◆ (L. 16)　**Now growth is weaker, ...**　（後続部で is が 2 か所で省略されていることに注意）
- ◆ (L. 17-18)　**Bank of Japan**　日本銀行
- ◆ (L. 19)　**outfit**　会社、機関
- ◆ (L. 19-20)　**Organization for Economic Cooperation and Development**　経済協力開発機構（OECD、正式英文名：Organisation for Economic Co-operation and Development。先進工業国を中心とした経済政策の調整を目指す国際機関。2016 年現在の加盟国は 34 ヵ国。本部：仏パリ）
- ◆ (L. 20)　**self-sabotage**　自己破壊行為
- ◆ (L. 22)　**primary budget surplus**　基礎的財政収支（primary balance）の黒字［税収などの正味の歳入（国債発行による借金を除く）と歳出（国債の元利払いを除く）の収支で国家財政の健全性の指標となる）］ primary deficit は基礎的財政収支赤字
- ◆ (L. 23)　**tank**　挫く、挫折させる
- ◆ (L. 24)　**International Monetary Fund**　国際通貨基金（略称 IMF。国際金融と為替相場の安定化を目指す国連の専門機関。2018 年現在の加盟国 189 カ国。本部：米ワシントン D.C.）
- ◆ (L. 24)　**Olivier Blanchard**　オリビエ・ブランシャール［Peterson Institute for International Economics（ピーターソン国際経済研究所）上席研究員。同研究所は、国際経済問題について分析・政策提言を行う米国の無党派シンクタンク］
- ◆ (L. 25)　**Takeshi Tashiro**　田代毅（ピーターソン国際研究所客員研究員）
- ◆ (L. 31)　**fiscal austerity**　財政緊縮策
- ◆ (L. 33)　**pre-financial crisis peak**　財政危機前のピーク時（ギリシャ政府による財政赤字の過少申告が発覚し、同国の国債価格が暴落したのが 2009 年秋。2000 年代の GDP 成長率はほぼ 3 〜 5 ％台で推移していたが、財政危機後は 2016 年頃までほぼ一貫してマイナス成長に陥った）

1. 本文の内容と一致するものには T (True) を、一致しないものには F (False) を記せ。

(　　　) (1) The article says in the first paragraph that Japan's economy would most likely be damaged unnecessarily if the sales-tax hike were not introduced.

(　　　) (2) A high level of general government deficits plays a role in the ruling party's commitment to raise the sales tax to 10 percent.

(　　　) (3) The Nikkei newspaper is cited as predicting that a lower house election will not be held along with the scheduled upper house election.

(　　　) (4) Since the early 1990s, Japan's Topix stock index has recorded an unmatched rise internationally.

(　　　) (5) The current weak performance of the Japanese economy is seen as a direct consequence of the sales tax increases in 2014 and thereafter.

2. 次の英文を完成させるために、(a) ～ (d) から最も適切なものを 1 つ選べ。

(1) The OECD supports the Japanese government's plan to raise the consumption tax to 10 percent, because_____
   (a) the country's general government deficit is already serious enough to justify a consumption tax of even 20 percent–26 percent.
   (b) it believes that the country should commit fiscal self-sabotage to stop itself from running up such huge fiscal deficits.
   (c) the country's primary budget surplus would reach 20 percent–26 percent without a cut in budget deficits.
   (d) a primary budget surplus as much as 20–26 percent would tank the country's economy.

(2) The article emphasizes the importance of economic growth in eliminating budget deficits, because_____
   (a) not a few countries succeeded in shrinking budget deficits by fiscal austerity.
   (b) much evidence is available that economic growth plays a major role in cutting deficits.
   (c) Greece slashed fiscal deficits and now enjoys a record-high economic growth.
   (d) the budget deficit reduction of almost a quarter always allows economies to prosper.

Natural
(10)
Slow
(12)

    A strategy by Chinese policymakers to stimulate the economy with tax and fee cuts hasn't stopped growth from slowing, stoking expectations that Beijing will roll out more incentives such as easier credit conditions to (1) ....

....

    Chinese economic growth slipped to 6.2 percent in the April-through-June quarter, (2) .... , after holding steady at 6.4 percent in the previous two quarters, official statistics showed Monday.

Natural
(11)
Slow
(13)

    Barring a modest recovery in June, signs accumulated that business activity struggled to pick up in the quarter. Consumer spending, which Chinese leaders hoped would support growth, is adding to the picture of cooling demand. The breakdown of second-quarter figures shows how roughly 2 trillion yuan ($291 billion) of stimulus, introduced by Premier Li Keqiang in March, is failing to (3) ....

    "I wouldn't say it's not working, but it's (4) .... people thought," said Bo Zhuang, an economist at research firm TS Lombard.

    The trade dispute with the US is dragging on China's economy and creating an uncertain business environment. To avoid the latest round of President Trump's tariffs, some manufacturers are (5) .... , fueling worries about layoffs and declining demand.

— Based on a report on WSJ.com —

5

10

15

〈ニュース解説〉　中国経済の成長鈍化が顕著になっている。直接的な要因として挙げられているのが米中貿易戦争による輸出の低迷、企業の投資意欲の減退、消費者心理の冷え込みである。2019年4-6月期のGDP成長率6.2%は、リーマンショック直後の2009年1-3月期の6.4%を下回り、1992年にこの統計数値の発表が始まって以来、最も低いレベルとなった。中国政府は景気失速を避けるために対策を強化すると見られているが、中国の債務残高は2018年6月末時点で既にGDPの254%に達しており、どこまで踏み込んだ対策が打たれるか注目されている。

(Notes)

policymaker 政策策定者　**tax and fee cuts** 企業に対する減税や社会保険料負担の軽減　**stoke** 掻き立てる、増長させる　**Beijing** 中国政府（首都名で当該政府を表すニュース英語の用法）　**easier credit** 金融緩和　**barring**（except for と同義）　**business activity** 経済活動　**consumer spending** 個人消費　**stimulus** 景気刺激策　**Premier Li Keqiang** 李克強首相　**Bo Zhuang** 荘伯　**TS Lombard** TS ロンバード（英国の調査会社）　**drag on ...** …を停滞させる　**latest round of President Trump's tariffs** 米トランプ政権による最新（第4弾）の追加関税　**layoff** 解雇

VOCABULARY BUILDUP

■問A 空所 (a) ～ (s) にそれぞれ入るべき1語を下記の語群から選びその番号を記せ。

国内総生産 → (a) domestic product
消費者物価指数 → (b) price index
卸売物価指数 → (c) price index
非関税障壁 → non-tariff (d)
最恵国 → most (e) nation
政府開発援助 → (f) development assistance
貿易不均衡 → trade (g)
為替レート → (h) rate
国際収支 → (i) of international payments
経常収支 → current (j)
貿易自由化 → trade (k)
社会保障 → social (l)
企業の合併・買収 → (m) and acquisition
株式公開買い付け → (n) bid
店頭取引株 → over-the-(o) stock
優良株 → (p) chip
不良債権 → (q) loan
失業率 → (r) rate
住宅着工件数 → (s) starts

1. account　　2. bad　　3. balance　　4. barrier
5. blue　　6. consumer　　7. counter　　8. exchange
9. favored　　10. gross　　11. housing　　12. imbalance
13. jobless　　14. liberalization　　15. merger　　16. official
17. security　　18. takeover　　19. wholesale

■問B (a) ～ (d) をそれぞれ和訳せよ。

(a) European Central Bank
(b) Bank of Japan
(c) Federal Reserve Board
(d) New York Stock Exchange

■問C (a) ～ (d) にそれぞれ対応する英語を下記の語群から選びその番号を記せ。

(a) 景気後退　　(b) 好況　　(c) 倒産　　(d) 年金

1. bankruptcy　　2. bonus　　3. boom　　4. breakdown
5. pension　　6. recession　　7. rehabilitation

The headline —「見出し」の特徴

現代英文ジャーナリズムの「見出し」(headline) では、日常的に用いられない語を「見出し語」(headlinese) として使用することを避ける傾向が強い。見出しは記事の内容を簡潔明瞭に表現する必要があり、一般的に次の5つの特徴を有している。

（1）略語が多い。例えば、"GOP" と言えば "Grand Old Party" の略称で、米国共和党 (Republican Party) の異名。

（2）特殊記号がある。例えば、"and" をカンマで代用したり、情報源を表すコロンがある。ヘッドラインのコロンはすべて情報源を表すものではないが、"Gunman in Manhattan kills one woman, wounds three: NYPD" とあれば、カンマは "and" に置き換えて "Gunman in Manhattan kills one woman and wounds three" となり、この情報は NYPD (New York City Police Department, ニューヨーク市警察) によってもたらされたことがわかる。

（3）冠詞や be 動詞は省略されることが多い。

（4）見出しにとどまらず、英語ニュースでは、首都名はその国や政府を表すことが多い。例えば、Washington は米国や米国政府を表す場合がよくある。もちろん首都自体のことを表す場合もあるから、文脈に注意。

（5）時制のずらしに気をつけよう。昨日起こったことでも現在形で表現。未来は to 不定詞で表現。例えば見出し語で "Government to regulate the Internet" とあれば、"the government will regulate the Internet" の意味。

このトピックを英文で読んでみよう。

The modern headline is distinguished by the fact that it says something—it makes a complete statement instead of merely characterizing. But, in addition, it speaks a language of its own. This language is not "headlinese," a perverted speech, but is merely pure English adapted to the requirements of headlining.

For one thing, the present tense is customarily used to describe past events. This usage is not something created by headline writers, but is simply something borrowed from everyday speech. The present tense is employed because it is the tense of immediacy, because it is more vivid and, hence, because it makes our trial tube of toothpaste inviting to the prospective buyer.

Another characteristic, which is more obvious to the ordinary reader, is the omission of non-essential words, chiefly articles. This practice has a tendency to give the headline telegraphic speed and, hence, to make it more vivid.

Still another characteristic of headline language is the use of short words, mainly of Anglo-Saxon derivation. And, here again, the space requirement is the commanding factor.

NEWS 3

Disk 1
(14)

Trump, China's Xi talk as trade war faces critical junction

A trade war between two economic titans faced a critical junction early Saturday, as President Donald Trump met with China's Xi Jinping as both sides signaled a desire to de-escalate the year-long conflict despite doubts about either side's willingness to compromise.

Taking place on the sidelines of the Group of 20 summit in Japan, the meeting ⁵ was the centerpiece of four days of diplomacy for Trump, whose re-election chances have been put at risk by the trade war that has both hurt American farmers and battered global markets. Tensions rose in recent weeks after negotiations collapsed last month and the two sides levied intensifying eye-for-an-eye punishments.

"We've had an excellent relationship," Trump told Xi as the meeting opened, "but ¹⁰ we want to do something that will even it up with respect to trade."

Seated across a wide table flanked by top aides, both leaders struck a cautiously optimistic tone after greeting each other and posing for photographs.

"I think this can be a very productive meeting. And I think we can go on to do something that will be truly monumental and great for both countries," Trump said. ¹⁵

(15) Xi, for his part, recounted the era of "ping-pong diplomacy," which helped jump-start US-China relations two generations ago. He said that, since then, "one basic fact remains unchanged: China and the United States both benefit from cooperation and lose in confrontation."

"Cooperation and dialogue are better than friction and confrontation," he added. ²⁰

The diplomacy plays out as Trump's re-election campaign battle is beginning to heat up, a contest that could be partially defined by whether a resolution to the trade war with China can be found before more economic pain is inflicted on Americans.

The president has threatened to impose tariffs on an additional $300 billion in Chinese imports — on top of the $250 billion in goods he's already taxed — ²⁵ extending his import taxes to virtually everything China ships to the United States. He has said the new tariffs, which are paid by US importers and usually passed onto consumers, might start at 10 percent. Earlier, the administration had said additional tariffs might reach 25 percent.

— Based on an AP report on registerguard.com —

〈ニュース解説〉　米トランプ政権は中国による知的財産権侵害（海外企業に中国への進出と引き換えに技術開示を強いる等）、為替操作（人民元の切り下げ）、資本移動の制限（海外企業による利益の国外送金の制限）等の撤廃を求めて、2018年7月〜2019年5月の間に2500億ドル（約27.5兆円）相当の中国製品に対して25％の追加関税を段階的に導入した。一方、中国も1100億ドル相当の米国製品に対し報復関税を課した（内500億ドルが25％、600億ドルが最大で10％の関税率）。2018年の中国の対米輸出額が5395億ドル、米国の対中輸出額が1203億ドルであることから、追加関税の規模の大きさが理解される。本ニュースが報じる米中首脳会談前に、米国はさらに3000億ドル相当の中国製品に最大で25％の追加関税の発動を示唆した。しかし、こう着状態に陥っていた貿易交渉を再開することで合意に達し、3000億ドルの追加関税の導入はとりあえず見送られた。

(Notes)

◆ (L. 1)　**titan**　巨大な人、大国
◆ (L. 2)　**President Donald Trump**　ドナルド・トランプ（米国）大統領
◆ (L. 2)　**Xi Jinping**　習近平（中国）国家主席
◆ (L. 3)　**the year-long conflict**　1年におよぶ（2国間の）対立

時期	米国	追加関税率	時期	中国	追加関税率
2018年7月6日	第1弾発動 340億米ドル相当の中国製品	25％	2018年7月6日	対抗措置発動 340億米ドル相当の米国製品	25％
2018年8月23日	第2弾発動 160億米ドル相当の中国製品	25％	2018年8月23日	対抗措置発動 160億米ドル相当の米国製品	25％
2018年9月24日	第3弾発動 2000億米ドル相当の中国製品	10％	2018年9月24日	対抗措置発動 600億米ドル相当の米国製品	最大10％
2019年5月10日	第3弾（2000億米ドル相当）の関税率引き上げ	25％	2019年5月13日	対抗措置公表（600億米ドル相当。6月1日以降引き上げ）	最大25％
2019年5月13日	第4弾を公表（約3000億米ドル相当の中国製品（2019年6月下旬以降発動）	最大25％			

『米中貿易摩擦の動向（2019年5月17日改訂版）』

◆ (L. 5)　**on the sidelines of …**　…の合間をぬって
◆ (L. 5)　**Group of 20 summit**　20カ国・地域首脳会合（G20サミット）［正式名称は「金融世界経済に関する首脳会合」（英語：Summit on Financial Markets and the World Economy）］
◆ (L. 9)　**(an) eye for an eye**　目には目を
◆ (L. 11)　**even it up**　（2国間の）関係を公平にする（it は relationship を指す）
◆ (L. 16)　**"ping-pong diplomacy"**　「ピンポン外交」（米中の国交は中華人民共和国が成立した1949年以降断絶していたが、1971年に日本で開催された世界卓球選手権における米中の卓球選手団の交流をきっかけに、米国選手団が北京に招待されたことから関係改善が始まり、1972年のニクソン米大統領の中国公式訪問へとつながったことを指す）
◆ (L. 16-17)　**jump-start**　急発進させる、活性化させる
◆ (L. 17)　**two generations ago**　2世代前（1世代は25〜30年なので、2世代前は約50年前）
◆ (L. 22)　**define**　決定付ける

1. 本文の内容と一致するものには T (True) を、一致しないものには F (False) を記せ。

   (   ) (1) At the summit meeting in Osaka, the two leaders eased rising tensions by compromising on bilateral trade issues.

   (   ) (2) Presidents Trump and Xi met for four days to resolve trade conflicts, which testifies to the importance of the trade relations between the two countries.

   (   ) (3) Mr. Trump called the relationship between the US and China "excellent" thanks to their mutually beneficial trade relationship.

   (   ) (4) In their discussions, Mr. Trump and Mr. Xi sounded hopeful about resolving their bilateral trade problems despite encountering possible difficulties.

   (   ) (5) President Xi's comments at the summit reflected the US-China relations that were now more characterized by confrontation than cooperation.

2. 次の英文を完成させるために、(a) 〜 (d) から最も適切なものを 1 つ選べ。

   (1) Judging from Mr. Xi's statement at the summit, the positions of the US and China amid escalating trade tensions can be most aptly described as _____

      (a) both the US and China having a lot to lose.

      (b) China having a lot more to lose than the US.

      (c) neither the US nor China having much to lose.

      (d) the US having far more to lose than China.

   (2) According to the article, China's annual exports of goods to the US roughly amount to _____

      (a) $250 billion

      (b) $300 billion

      (c) $550 billion

      (d) (no indication in the article)

Natural
16

Slow
18

　　US Federal Reserve Chairman Jerome Powell is suggesting short-term interest rates could soon be cut as the global economy weakens and concerns persist over trade policy.

　　As he delivered the Fed's semi-annual monetary report to Congress Wednesday, Powell signaled the central bank might cut interest rates [(1)] ＿＿＿＿＿＿＿ 5 nearly a decade. Powell said, "uncertainties around trade tensions and concerns about the strength of the global economy continue to [(2)] ＿＿＿＿＿＿＿

＿＿＿＿＿＿＿."

Natural
17

Slow
19

　　He told the House Financial Services Committee the cuts could come when Fed officials meet later this month. Powell said, while [(3)] ＿＿＿＿＿＿＿ 10

＿＿＿＿＿＿＿ and consumer spending has been stable, the business investment growth rate has "slowed notably."

　　He also noted that slower growth by some large foreign economies "could affect the US economy." The Fed's benchmark rate is currently [(4)] ＿＿＿＿＿＿＿

＿＿＿＿＿＿＿ and some market observers predict the central bank will cut it by a 15 quarter percentage point.

　　Trump, who is relying on a strong economy to help propel him to a second term in office next year, has called the Fed his biggest threat. Trump attacked the Fed when it increased rates four times last year, [(5)] ＿＿＿＿＿＿＿

＿＿＿＿＿＿＿ and depressed the stock market. 20

— Based on a report on VOANews.com —

〈ニュース解説〉　米連邦準備理事会（FRB）が 2019 年 7 月末に 10 年半振りの利下げに踏み切った。下げ幅は本記事が予測しているように 0.25% となった。米景気は失業率も低く、個人消費も力強い中、現時点での利上げの必要性を問う見方もある。しかし、米中の貿易戦争や世界景気の減速懸念で企業投資が弱含んでおり、予防的な利下げとの見方が一般的である。

(Notes)
US Federal Reserve chairman 米連邦準備理事会議長（Federal Reserve（Board））は米国の中央銀行）　**Jerome Powell** ジェローム・パウエル　**short-term interest rate** 短期金利［ここでは政策金利の「フェデラル・ファンド金利」（Federal Funds Rate）を意味し、連邦公開市場委員会（Federal Open Market Committee、略称 FOMC）で決定される］　**Fed's semi-annual monetary report to Congress** 連邦準備理事会が年 2 回議会に提出する金融政策報告書（Fed は Federal Reserve Board の略称）　**House Financial Services Committee** 米議会下院金融サービス委員会［House は House of Representative（米国下院）の意味］　**benchmark rate** 政策金利（中央銀行が市中銀行融資する際の金利で景気に応じて景気が良い場合には高く、悪い場合には低く設定される）　**percentage point** パーセンテージ・ポイント

■問A　空所 (a) 〜 (s) にそれぞれ入るべき１語を下記の語群から選びその番号を記せ。

グローバル人材	→	globally (a) human resources
重厚長大産業	→	(b) industry
終身雇用	→	(c) employment
熟練労働者	→	(d) worker
年功序列昇進制度	→	(e)-based promotion system
能力主義昇進制度	→	(f)-based promotion system
食料自給率	→	food (g)-sufficiency rate
初任給	→	(h) salary
人材派遣会社	→	(i)-employment agency
数値目標	→	(j) target
正社員	→	(k) employee
契約社員	→	(l) employee
設備投資	→	(m) investment
先行指標	→	(n) indicator
遅行指標	→	(o) indicator
一致指標	→	(p) indicator
知的所有権	→	intellectual (q) rights
確定給付型年金	→	defined-(r) pension plan
確定拠出型年金	→	defined-(s) pension plan

1. benefit	2. capital	3. coincident	4. competitive
5. contract	6. contribution	7. full-time	8. lagging
9. leading	10. lifetime	11. numerical	12. performance
13. property	14. self	15. seniority	16. skilled
17. smokestack	18. starting	19. temporary	

■問B　(a) 〜 (d) をそれぞれ和訳せよ。

(a) Asian Infrastructure Investment Bank

(b) Government Pension Investment Fund, Japan

(c) Japan External Trade Organization

(d) National Federation of Agricultural Cooperative Associations

■問C　(a) 〜 (d) にそれぞれ対応する英語表現を下記の語群から選びその番号を記せ。

(a) 格安航空会社　　(b) 投資収益率　　(c) 有効求人倍数　　(d) 連結決算

1. consolidated earnings	2. effective labor force	3. low-cost carrier
4. ratio of job offers to seekers	5. return on investment	6. ultra-low airfare

THE WORLD OF ENGLISH JOURNALISM

The inverted pyramid ― 逆ピラミッドとは

英文のニュースの大半は、ハード・ニュース（hard news）と呼ばれ、経済・政治・犯罪・事故・災害などに関連して日々起こる重要な出来事をスピーディーかつ簡潔に読者に伝える内容となっている。新聞の読者、テレビやラジオの視聴者、さらにはインターネットの利用者にとって時間は最も貴重な資源であり、多くの人たちは限られた時間内に最大限の情報を入手する必要に迫られている。こうしたニーズに対応するために考案されたのが逆ピラミッド型と呼ばれるニュースの構成であり、Chapter 6で紹介するフィーチャー・ニュース（feature news）の構成と対比される。

このトピックを英文で読んでみよう。

This news writing format summarizes the most important facts at the very start of the story. It may seem like an obvious idea to us nowadays—getting right to the point when you start a story—but it didn't occur to most reporters until midway through the 19th century. What changed? Sentences got shorter. Writing got tighter. And reporters developed a formula for compressing the most newsworthy facts—the who, what, when, where, why—into the opening paragraphs of a story. That formula lives on today. It's known as the inverted pyramid.

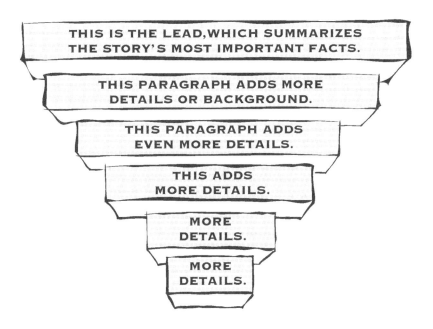

THIS IS THE LEAD, WHICH SUMMARIZES THE STORY'S MOST IMPORTANT FACTS.

THIS PARAGRAPH ADDS MORE DETAILS OR BACKGROUND.

THIS PARAGRAPH ADDS EVEN MORE DETAILS.

THIS ADDS MORE DETAILS.

MORE DETAILS.

MORE DETAILS.

NEWS 4

Trump begins state visit to Japan

(20) U.S. President Donald Trump has arrived in Japan for a four-day state visit heavy on ceremony and sports, although a senior White House official promises "there'll be some substantive things to announce."

Trump went directly from the airport on Saturday evening to the U.S. ambassador's official residence to address several dozen top Japanese business leaders. 5

"The relationship with Japan and the United States I can say for a fact has never been stronger, never been more powerful, never been closer," the president told the executives.

Trump expressed hope the United States and Japan will soon be able to reach a new trade pact. 10

"Japan has had a substantial advantage for many, many years, but that's OK, maybe that's why you like us so much," said Trump, adding that the trade imbalance strongly in Japan's favor for decades would become "a little bit more fair."

(21) The overall visit, however, will focus more on photo opportunities rather than deal-making and that may be intentional on the part of Japanese Prime Minister 15 Shinzo Abe, who has forged a close relationship with Trump. The two have met or spoken more than 40 times, which is "absolutely unprecedented," according to the White House.

The president is to attend a banquet with the new emperor, golf with the prime minister and view the ancient sport of sumo – awarding what has been nicknamed the 20 "Trump Cup" to a champion wrestler.

One goal of Abe's during their time together in Tokyo is to ensure Trump is committed to next month's Group of 20 leaders summit Japan will host in Osaka.

Trump on Monday meets with Emperor Naruhito and attends a state banquet. The U.S. president is Japan's first formal guest of the Reiwa era, which began May 25 1 with the new monarch ascending to the Chrysanthemum Throne, succeeding his elderly father, Akihito, who abdicated.

Trump and Abe on Tuesday are to inspect a Japan Maritime Self-Defense Force helicopter carrier at the Yokosuka naval base, putting the final focus for the president's visit on the close military relationship between the two countries, which were on 30 opposing sides during World War II.

— Based on a report on VOANews.com —

〈ニュース解説〉　新天皇即位後、令和初の国賓として、ドナルド・トランプ米国大統領が訪日した。世界の指導者の中で最も頻繁にコンタクトを取っている安倍晋三首相と親交を深めることで、北朝鮮問題などへの連携強化を図ることが主要な目的。日米貿易交渉等を除けば、二国間で大きな懸案もない中、友好ムードに終始した。

(Notes)

◆ **Trump begins state visit to Japan**　トランプ大統領　国賓として来日［"state visit" は国家元首などが「他国を正式に（国賓として）訪問すること」。「国賓（state guest）」に対しては、国と国との付き合いの観点で、最高度のもてなしをする。年間に数人しか対象にならず、通常は、より簡易な「公賓（official guest）」扱いとすることが多い］

◆ (L. 2)　**ceremony and sports**　（外交）儀礼とスポーツ（天皇陛下によるもてなしや首脳同士のゴルフ、大相撲観戦などを指す）

◆ (L. 2)　**a senior White House official**　大統領府のある高官［ここでの "White House" は、大統領官邸内で大統領をサポートするため、補佐官等のスタッフが常駐する大統領府（the Executive Office of the President）を指す。後出の "White House" も同旨。ニュースソースの明示を避けるため、不詳、不明を表す不定冠詞 "a" を使っている］

◆ (L. 4-5)　**the U.S. ambassador's official residence**　駐日米国大使公邸（東京・赤坂の米国大使館に隣接する）

◆ (L. 5)　**several dozen top Japanese business leaders**　数十人の日本の経済界トップ（"dozen" は1ダースで12の意。通常単複同形。"several dozen" は36以上との定義もある）

◆ (L. 10)　**a new trade pact**　新たな貿易協定［トランプ大統領主導で開始された日米貿易交渉を踏まえ、締結が見込まれる協定を指す。今回の日米交渉について、日本政府は物品を中心とした物品貿易協定（Trade Agreement on Goods, TAG）であるとしているが、米国政府は、包括的な自由貿易協定（Free Trade Agreement, FTA）を含む日米貿易協定と位置付けている］

◆ (L. 11)　**substantial advantage**　（貿易における）実質的な有利性（日本の市場が閉鎖的であるため競争条件が日本側に有利であるという説。1980年代の日米貿易摩擦開始以来の米側の主張）

◆ (L. 12-13)　**trade imbalance strongly in Japan's favor**　日本側に有利な貿易不均衡（日本側が常に輸出超過であるとの意）

◆ (L. 13)　**"a little bit more fair"**　少々公正に（不均衡の原因が不公正な日本の貿易慣行にあるとする前提に基づいている）

◆ (L. 14)　**photo opportunities**　（報道陣による、儀礼的な）写真撮影の機会

◆ (L. 15)　**intentional**　意図的な

◆ (L. 17)　**"absolutely unprecedented"**　まったく異例なこと、前例がないこと

◆ (L. 19)　**banquet with the new emperor**　新天皇主催の宮中晩さん会（後掲の "state banquet" も同義）

◆ (L. 20)　**the ancient sport of sumo**　日本古来の国技である大相撲（"of" は同格を表す）

◆ (L. 21)　**the "Trump Cup"**　「トランプカップ（杯）」（高さ137㎝、重さ30kg。正式名称「アメリカ合衆国大統領杯」を指す）

◆ (L. 21)　**champion wrestler**　優勝力士（英語では相撲は "Sumo wrestling" 力士は "Sumo wrestler" と呼ばれる）

◆ (L. 23)　**Group of 20 leaders summit**　G20首脳会合（翌2019年6月の大阪開催が予定されていた）

◆ (L. 24)　**Emperor Naruhito**　（徳仁）天皇陛下（Chapter 7 News 7 参照）

◆ (L. 25)　**Japan's first formal guest of the Reiwa era**　令和時代初となる日本の国賓

◆ (L. 26)　**the new monarch ascending to the Chrysanthemum Throne**　皇位につかれた新天皇陛下（"the Chrysanthemum Throne" の直訳は「菊の皇位」となるが、日本の皇室が菊のご紋を使っていることから英語圏ではこう呼ばれる）

◆ (L. 27)　**elderly father, Akihito**　父親の（明仁）上皇陛下（Chapter 7 News 7 参照）

◆ (L. 28-29)　**Japan Maritime Self-Defense Force helicopter carrier**　海上自衛隊のヘリコプター搭載護衛艦「かが」を指す（「かが」については、Chapter 5 News 5 参照）

◆ (L. 29)　**Yokosuka naval base**　（海上自衛隊）横須賀基地（正式には「海上自衛隊横須賀地方隊」と呼ぶ。海上自衛隊は海軍ではないが、国際ニュース等では海軍を表す "navy" に擬されることや、米海軍第7艦隊が常駐することから、「海軍基地」を意味する "naval base" が使われている）

◆ (L. 31)　**opposing sides during World War II**　第2次世界大戦中は敵対していた

1. 本文の内容と一致するものには T (True) を、一致しないものには F (False) を記せ。

(　　) (1) A high-ranking official in the presidential office said President Trump's visit to Japan would be not only ceremonial but also substantive.

(　　) (2) Upon his arrival in Tokyo, President Trump went directly to the US Ambassador's official residence for a rest.

(　　) (3) At the meeting with Japanese business leaders, Mr. Trump complained about Japan's unfair practices in trade but made little demand for the country's effort to improve them.

(　　) (4) President Trump expressed his desire to strike a new trade agreement with Japan soon.

(　　) (5) Prime Minister Abe seemed indifferent to substantive issues such as getting an assurance from President Trump on his commitment to the G20 summit to be held in Osaka.

2. ドナルド・トランプ米国大統領の訪日について説明した次の英文について、空欄 (1) ～ (6) に入るべき語を、下記語群 (a) ～ (j) の中から選んで記せ。

President Donald Trump became the first (　1　) of state to make an (　2　) visit to Japan since its (　3　) era name changed to Reiwa with the new Emperor's (　4　). Both President Trump and Prime Minister Abe emphasized the strength of the diplomatic (　5　) and the friendship between the two countries, concentrating not on deal-making but on (　6　) opportunities.

(a) accession　(b) descending　(c) geological　(d) head　(e) imperial
(f) official　(g) secret　(h) social　(i) tale　(j) ties

音声を聞き、下線部を補え。（２回録音されています。１回目はナ
チュラルスピード、２回目はスロースピードです。）

Natural
🔊 22

Slow
🔊 24

    Group of 20 leaders have clearly confirmed the need for a free, fair and non-discriminatory trade policy, Japanese Prime Minister Shinzo Abe said on Saturday, suggesting that members have agreed to the wording [1] _____.

    Speaking after chairing the two-day G20 summit in Osaka, western Japan, Abe said the leaders also found [2] _____ despite "big differences" in the members' views.

    "The global economy continues to face downside risks as trade tensions persist," Abe told a news conference.

Natural
🔊 23

Slow
🔊 25

    "The G20 leaders agreed on the need for member countries [3] _____," while standing ready to take further action if needed, he said.

    Abe also said he had told U.S. President Donald Trump and Chinese President Xi Jinping that it was extremely important [4] _____ to solve their trade tensions.

    The United States and China have agreed to restart trade talks and Washington will not level new tariffs on Chinese exports, China's official Xinhua news agency reported, as Trump said the talks were "back on track."

    "The G20 agreed on fundamental principles backing a free trade system, which is to ensure free, fair, non-discriminatory trade, as well as open markets and [5] _____," Abe said.

— Based on a report on Reuters.com —

〈ニュース解説〉　初めて日本で開催された G20 サミット（首脳会合）。米中の「貿易戦争」が自由貿易体制に影を落とす中、議長国日本は、取りまとめに奔走した。場外で並行して行われた各国首脳による二国間会談では、米中間の貿易問題に一定の前進も見られるなどの成果もあった。

(Notes)

Group of 20 leaders G20 首脳［G20（Group of Twenty）は先進国からなる G7（日、米、英、独、仏、伊、加）、BRICS（ブラジル、ロシア、インド、中国、南ア）の他、メキシコ、豪州、韓国、インドネシア、サウジアラビア、トルコ、アルゼンチンの 19 か国と EU からなる。2008 年のリーマンショックを機に "G20 Summit（金融・世界経済に関する首脳会合）" として開始された。G7 が政治・安全保障・経済に関する包括的な西側諸国の首脳会合なのに対し、議題は経済問題に限定されている］　**free, fair and non-discriminatory trade policy** 自由で公正かつ無差別な貿易政策［GATT（General Agreement on Tariffs and Trade 関税と貿易に関する一般協定）や同協定の実施機関である WTO（世界貿易機関）に象徴される自由貿易体制の原則を指す］　**chairing** 議長を務める　**downside risks** 下振れリスク　**trade tensions** 貿易上の緊張関係（米中貿易摩擦を指す）　**Washington** 米国政府を指す　**level new tariffs on Chinese exports** 中国製品に新たに関税を賦課する　**China's official Xinhua news agency** 中国国営新華社通信　**back on track** 元の軌道に戻る

■問A　空所 (a) ～ (f) にそれぞれ入るべき 1 語を下記の語群から選びその番号を記せ。

国連総会（UNGA）　　　　　　→　United Nations General (a)
国連安全保障理事会（UNSC）　→　United Nations Security (b)
国連難民高等弁務官（UNHCR）→　United Nations High (c) for Refugees
国連食糧農業機関（FAO）　　　→　(United Nations) Food and Agriculture (d)
国際原子力機関（IAEA）　　　→　International Atomic Energy (e)
国際通貨基金（IMF）　　　　　→　International Monetary (f)

　　1. Agency　　2. Assembly　　3. Commissioner　　4. Council
　　5. Forum　　6. Fund　　7. Operation　　8. Organization

■問B　(a) ～ (k) にそれぞれ入るべき 1 語を下記の語群から選びその番号を記せ。

国連教育科学文化機関（UNESCO）→　United Nations (a) Scientific and Cultural Organization
国際労働機関（ILO）　　　　→　International (b) Organization
世界保健機関（WHO）　　　　→　World (c) Organization
世界貿易機関（WTO）　　　　→　World (d) Organization
国際復興開発銀行（IBRD）　→　International Bank for (e) and Development
アジア太平洋経済協力（APEC）→　Asia-Pacific (f) Cooperation
東南アジア諸国連合（ASEAN）→　(g) of Southeast Asian Nations
北大西洋条約機構（NATO）　→　North Atlantic (h) Organization
石油輸出国機構（OPEC）　　→　Organization of the (i) Exporting Countries
経済協力開発機構（OECD）　→　Organisation for Economic (j) and Development
国際エネルギー機関（IEA）　→　International (k) Agency

　　1. Association　　2. Co-operation　　3. Countries　　4. Economic
　　5. Educational　　6. Energy　　7. Healing　　8. Health
　　9. Labor　　10. Leaders　　11. Petroleum　　12. Power
　　13. Reconstruction　　14. Rehabilitation　　15. Trade　　16. Treaty

■問C　(a) ～ (g) をそれぞれ和訳せよ。

(a) Ambassador Extraordinary and Plenipotentiary
(b) diplomatic immunity
(c) ratification
(d) sovereignty
(e) COP
(f) exile
(g) economic sanctions

The lead ― リードの役割

すべてのニュースがこの形をとるわけではないが、特に "hard news" は、リードと呼ばれる導入部でニュースの要約を伝えるのが普通である。一般に five W's and one H のすべての要素が、最初の1〜2の段落に凝縮される。「lead（リード）」は「headline（見出し）」のすぐ後に書かれ、リードの後に続くのが「body（本文）」である。ヘッドラインはスペース上の問題もあり記事の内容を正確に伝えきれないこともあるが、リードは記事の内容を冒頭で要約して、読者に端的に伝える。

このトピックを英文で読んでみよう。

A news story has two main parts: a lead and a body.

Usually the lead is the opening paragraph but may include the second and third paragraphs as well. It is the essence of the news as presented in summary form at the beginning of the story.

A typical lead is:

Telephone wires leading into 15 dwellings were cut yesterday afternoon, apparently by vandals, interrupting service for 25 users.

Leads have many constructions and patterns of their own. Generally, however, they seek to answer six questions about the news—Who? What? When? Where? Why? and How?

The body of the story is all the rest beyond the lead, no matter whether the remainder is three or 30 paragraphs long. The arrangement of the body often follows logically from the lead, but it, too, must be planned.

Suspect, Charged, Said to Admit to Role in Plot

By Mark Mazzetti, Sabrina Tavernise And Jack Healy

Lead

A Pakistani-American man arrested in the failed Times Square car bombing has admitted his role in the attempted attack and said he received explosives training in Pakistan, the authorities said Tuesday.

The man, Faisal Shahzad, 30, was arrested as he tried to flee the country in a Dubai-bound jet late Monday. Hours later, there were reports that seven or eight people had been arrested in Pakistan, as officials in both countries sought to

FBI search a house where Faisal Shahzad lived in Bridgeport, Conn., Tuesday, May 4, 2010.

confirmed, it would be the group's first effort to attack the United States and the first sign of the

booked a ticket on his way to Kennedy Airport and bought it with cash when he got there, officials

Officials said Mr. Shahzad had been placed on a no-fly list on Monday afternoon, but they declined to explain how he had been allowed to board the plane.
An Isuzu Trooper that Mr. Shahzad had apparently driven to the airport was found in a parking lot. Inside the Trooper, investigators discovered a Kel-Tec 9-millimeter pistol, with a folding stock and a rifle barrel, along with several spare magazines of ammunition, an official said. Fearing the Izuzu might be rigged to explode, officials briefly cordoned off the area around it.
All of the passengers were taken off the plane, and they, their luggage and the Boeing 777 were screened

before the flight w depart, about seven 6:29 a.m. Two other interviewed by the released, according enforcement officia said Mr. Shahza providing "useful i federal investigator pulled off the plane. that he had receiv Pakistan, Mr. Shah acted alone, a clain being investigated.
In Pakistan, unfolded quickl identified one of th Tauhid Ahmed an been in touch wit through e-mail and

NEWS 5

Disk 1

(26) **Japan to have first aircraft carriers since World War II**

Tokyo — Japan is poised to put its first aircraft carriers to sea since World War II, refitting its Izumo-class warships to carry US-designed F-35B fighter jets, the government announced Tuesday. In its 10-year Defense Program Guidelines, Tokyo said it will buy 42 of the stealthy F-35Bs, which are designed for short-run take offs and vertical landings. 5

Those planes will be available for deployment aboard two flat-top ships, the JS Izumo and JS Kaga, which at more than 800 feet long and displacing 27,000 tons are the largest ships in the Japanese fleet. "Under the drastically changing security environment around Japan, the government will take all possible measures to protect the lives and assets of Japanese people," Chief Cabinet Secretary Yoshihide Suga said 10 Tuesday in announcing the plan.

(27) The Izumo and Kaga have been carrying helicopters designed for anti-submarine warfare since entering service over the past three years. They will need to have their decks reinforced to accommodate the heavier F-35Bs, as well as the heat and force from the jets' thrusters when they land vertically. 15

Japan will also increase its order for F-35A jets, which take off and land on conventional runways, to 105, the government said. Forty-two of those jets are in service or were part of earlier Japanese orders. Those planes will replace the Japan Air Self-Defense Force's aging F-15J fighters.

Carl Schuster, a former director of operations at the US Pacific Command's 20 Joint Intelligence Center, said the new aircraft carriers would give Tokyo the ability to mount territory defenses farther out from its main islands. It comes after a Japanese defense white paper in August highlighted concerns about China. "China's rapid modernization of the People's Liberation Army, enhancement of operational capabilities, and unilateral escalation of activities in areas close to Japan 25 are generating strong security concerns in the region and international community, including Japan," the paper said.

— Based on a report on CNN.com —

〈ニュース解説〉　これから先 10 年程度を念頭に、中長期的視点で日本の安全保障体制や防衛力のあり方を定めた防衛計画大綱が発表された。大綱の目玉は、短距離滑走での離陸と垂直着陸が可能な F-35B 最新鋭ステルス戦闘機を米国から購入することと、同戦闘機を搭載するため「いずも」型護衛艦（現在はヘリコプター搭載護衛艦）の改装が盛り込まれていることである。このような高価な米国製最新鋭戦闘機の購入の背景には、日米貿易不均衡に不満を示すトランプ米大統領に対する配慮も垣間見ることができるが、同時に東シナ海や南シナ海海域での勢力拡大を加速させる中国を牽制する狙いがある。

(Notes)

◆ (L. 2)　**refitting its Izumo-class warships**　「いずも」型護衛艦の改装（現在のヘリコプター搭載護衛艦を戦闘機搭載可能な空母に改装すること。「いずも」型護衛艦は、それ以前に建造された「ひゅうが」型護衛艦を大型化したものであり、1 番艦の「いずも」と 2 番艦の「かが」がある）

◆ (L. 2)　**F-35B fighter jets**　F-35B ジェット戦闘機（ステルス性能を持つ最新鋭機。短距離離陸及び垂直着陸機能を有する。F-35 シリーズにはこのほか、後掲の "F-35A" という通常型がある）

◆ (L. 3)　**10-year Defense Program Guidelines**　今後 10 年の防衛計画大綱（この大綱は、今後概ね 10 年の防衛の基本方針や自衛隊の具体的体制の方針を示す）

◆ (L. 3)　**Tokyo**　（日本政府を指す）

◆ (L. 4)　**stealthy**　ステルスの（レーダー捕捉不能の）

◆ (L. 6)　**flat-top ships**　航空母艦（"aircraft carrier" のこと。口語表現では、単に "flattop" 或いは "carrier" とも称される）

◆ (L. 6-7)　**JS Izumo and JS Kaga**　護衛艦「いずも」及び「かが」[JS は Japan Ship の略で、海上自衛隊艦船の外国名に付けられる艦船接頭辞。米国海軍艦船には USS（United States Ship）、英国海軍艦船には HMS（Her 又は His Majesty's Ship）の艦船接頭辞が付く]

◆ (L. 7)　**displacing**　〜の排水量がある（浮かべた場合に、押しのける水の量で船の大きさを表す）

◆ (L. 10)　**Chief Cabinet Secretary Yoshihide Suga**　菅義偉内閣官房長官

◆ (L. 16)　**F-35A jets**　F-35A ジェット戦闘機

◆ (L. 18-19)　**Japan Air Self-Defense Force**　航空自衛隊

◆ (L. 19)　**F-15J fighters**　F-15J 戦闘機（米マクドネル・ダグラス社の F-15C/D を三菱重工等が日本仕様にノックダウン及びライセンス生産した。導入から既に 40 年近く経つが、現在も日本の主力戦闘機である）

◆ (L. 20-21)　**Carl Schuster, a former director of operations at the US Pacific Command's Joint Intelligence Center**　カール・シュスター米太平洋軍統合情報センター前作戦部長（太平洋軍は旧名称。2018 年 5 月からインド太平洋軍（US Indo-Pacific Command）へと名称変更がされている。インド洋はこれまでも米太平洋軍の作戦海域であったが、この名称変更には、同軍の作戦対象海域である南シナ海で軍事施設を建設し進出を加速させ、一帯一路構想（Belt and Road Initiative）でインド洋までも勢力を拡大しつつある中国を牽制する狙いがある）

◆ (L. 23)　**defense white paper**　防衛白書（防衛省が毎年刊行し、防衛政策の基本理念を掲げ、近隣諸国等の現状分析をもとにして各種政策提言を行っている）

◆ (L. 24)　**People's Liberation Army**　（中国）人民解放軍（中国共産党の軍事組織。国軍に相当する）

1. 本文の内容と一致するものには T (True) を、一致しないものには F (False) を記せ。

(   ) (1) Japan has never owned a flat-top in history.

(   ) (2) F-35B fighters will be used mostly for naval operations.

(   ) (3) F-35Bs need long runways for take-off.

(   ) (4) From the building stage, the decks of both the Izumo and the Kaga were reinforced to resist the heat created by vertical landings of F-35B fighters.

(   ) (5) From the Defense Ministry's point of view, F-15J fighters are still good enough to protect Japan's airspace from the possible foreign invasion in the future.

(   ) (6) The total number of F-35 (A & B) fighters Japan has promised to purchase from the US amounts to 147.

(   ) (7) With the refurbishment of the decks of the Izumo-class ships, the Japanese government admits that its Self-Defense Forces can act in an offensive role.

(   ) (8) China's rapid increase in military capabilities is viewed by Japan's defense community as its primary threat.

2. 次の英文を完成させるために、(a) ～ (d) から最も適切なものを 1 つ選べ。

China's attitude toward Japan's recent defense buildup in the wake of the possible purchase of F-35B fighters and the refit of the Izumo-class ships seems to be_____

(a) affirmative, as increased Japanese military spending certainly helps to maintain the military balance between the two major powers in East Asia.

(b) indifferent, as China still remains the dominant power in the region despite Japan's efforts to build up its naval power.

(c) critical, as the defensive nature of Japan's Self-Defense Forces may change as the result of these military buildups.

(d) accepting, as China does not see Japan's Self-Defense Forces as a major threat as long as they act within the framework of the US–Japan Security Treaty.

音声を聞き、下線部を補え。（２回録音されています。１回目はナチュラルスピード、２回目はスロースピードです。）

Natural
28

Slow
30

The US Navy sailed two destroyers through the Taiwan Strait on Sunday, (1)_____ a "routine" transit. "The ships' transit through the Taiwan Strait demonstrates the US commitment to a free and open Indo-Pacific," a spokesman for the Navy's Seventh Fleet told CNN in a statement. "The US Navy will continue to fly, (2)_____," he added. 5

The Trump administration has sought to make the Taiwan Strait transits more routine, with the operations now (3)_____. Prior to July, the transits occurred only about once a year.

Natural
29

Slow
31

The approximately 110-mile-wide strait, which separates the People's Republic of China and Taiwan, is seen as a potential geopolitical flashpoint should Beijing ever seek to (4)_____. 10

Taiwan accused China of "reckless and provocative" action after two Chinese air force jets (5)_____ separating the island from the mainland on March 31. The island's military scrambled fighter planes after two Chinese J-11 fighter jets crossed the border within the waters of the Taiwan Strait, known as the median line. 15

— *Based on a report on CNN.com* —

〈ニュース解説〉 2019年1月2日、蔡英文（さいえいぶん）台湾総統は、中国が求める一国二制度を台湾が受け入れることは絶対にないと明言したが、同じ日北京では、習近平中国国家主席が、「中華民族の偉大な復興へのプロセスにおいて台湾同胞を欠くことはありえない」と訴え、台湾に対する武力行使も選択肢にあるとの立場を表明している。このような中国の威嚇に対し、国交はないが台湾の同盟国である米国は台湾海峡に海軍艦艇を航行させ中国を牽制している。南シナ海で岩礁を占拠する中国に対し、米海軍艦船が中心になって、航行の自由を行動で示すいわゆる「航行の自由作戦」（freedom of navigation operations）が展開されているが、台湾海峡での米軍の動きもこのような示威作戦の１つと考えられる。

(Notes)
destroyer 駆逐艦　**Taiwan Strait** 台湾海峡　**routine transit** 通常の航行、通過（実際は中国に対する威嚇・示威行為であっても、国際法上認められている軍艦の単なる海峡通過であることを強調している）　**a free and open Indo-Pacific** 自由で開かれたインド・太平洋（戦略）。中国の一帯一路に対抗して、米日豪を中心に推進する戦略　**Seventh Fleet** 米国第7艦隊（ホノルルに司令部のある太平洋艦隊の指揮下で、西太平洋及びインド洋が担当海域）　**Beijing** 北京（ここでは中国或いは中国政府を指す）　**J-11 fighter jet** 殲（せん）11戦闘機（ロシアから輸入した複座型戦闘機で、中国の航空戦力の主軸の１つを占める）　**median line** 中間線

■問A 自衛隊関連用語 (a) 〜 (d) にそれぞれ入るべき1語を下記の語群から選びその番号を
　　　記せ。

自衛隊　　　　→　Japan Self-Defense (a)
陸上自衛隊　　→　Japan (b) Self-Defense Force
海上自衛隊　　→　Japan (c) Self-Defense Force
航空自衛隊　　→　Japan (d) Self-Defense Force

　　1. Air　　　2. Force　　　3. Forces　　　4. Ground　　　5. Maritime　　　6. Sea

■問B 米軍関連用語 (a) 〜 (e) をそれぞれ和訳せよ。

(a) United States Armed Forces
(b) United States Army
(c) United States Navy
(d) United States Air Force
(e) United States Marine Corps

■問C 軍事用語 (a) 〜 (d) をそれぞれ和訳せよ。

(a) anti-ballistic missile (ABM)
(b) airborne warning and control system (AWACS)
(c) intermediate-range ballistic missile (MRBM)
(d) Nuclear Non-Proliferation Treaty (NPT)

■問D (a) 〜 (j) にそれぞれ対応する英語表現を下記の語群から選びその番号を記せ。

(a) 平和維持活動　　(b) 非武装地帯　　(c) 文民統制　　(d) 核軍縮
(e) 核保有国　　　　(f) 通常兵器　　　(g) 地雷　　　　(h) 休戦
(i) 大量破壊兵器　　(j) 自爆テロ

1. ceasefire	2. civilian control
3. conventional weapons	4. demilitarized zone (DMZ)
5. landmine	6. nuclear disarmament
7. nuclear powers	8. peacekeeping operations
9. terrorist suicide bombing	10. weapons of mass destruction (WMD)

Beyond the basic news lead — 異なるスタイルのリード

社会問題や面白そうな人物を扱った記事等、解説的要素が大きく入り込む記事においては、前章で触れたような事実だけを並べた要約的なリードで記事を書き始めたのでは何とも味気ない。すべてのニュースが時宜を得たものであるとは限らない。昨日今日のニュースのように即時性が要求されるニュースでない場合は、もっと生き生きしたクリエイティヴで掘り下げた、場合によっては楽しく人をわくわくさせる記事の書き方が求められる。

このトピックを英文で読んでみよう。

It's not mandatory to begin every story with a roundup of essential facts. For most breaking news events, you need leads that are quick, factual and concise. You need leads that summarize the who-what-when-where-why. But not every story is a timely news event. Some stories explore social issues. Some profile interesting people. And for those, a basic news lead may be too dull and dry. You may need something livelier, snappier, more creative, a lead that doesn't just summarize, but amuses, astonishes and intrigues.

NEWS MEDIA IN THE WORLD

通信社　News Agencies (1)

✓ "news agency" や "news service" と呼ばれる「通信社」は、独自の取材陣又は国内外の報道機関などと連携し、作成したニュース記事を写真やビデオ映像などとともに新聞社、放送会社へ配信する組織。膨大な取材ネットワークが必要なため、単独の新聞社等では対応が困難なことから、報道機関が共同して通信社を設ける非営利型の組合組織も多い。

NEWS 6

Disk 1

Stepping into power, Johnson seeks more diverse Cabinet

Taking over as prime minister on Wednesday, Boris Johnson is expected to unveil a more diverse top team in a government to be tasked with delivering Brexit by the end of October, with or without a deal.

The former London mayor won the contest to succeed Theresa May on Tuesday by securing the leadership of the Conservative Party in a campaign that put the United Kingdom on course for a showdown with the European Union. 5

Johnson's Cabinet choices will help to flesh out how he intends to manage the world's fifth-largest economy and its divorce from the EU at one of the most fateful moments in its modern history.

"Boris will build a Cabinet showcasing all the talents within the party that truly 10 reflect modern Britain," a source close to Johnson said.

May will leave Downing Street later on Wednesday to hand in her resignation to the Queen, who will formally appoint Johnson.

With the pound stuck near two-year lows against the US dollar due to rising concerns about a "no-deal" Brexit, investors are braced to see who will be handed the 15 top roles such as Chancellor, foreign secretary and Brexit minister.

A record number of ethnic minority politicians are expected to serve as ministers, including Priti Patel, the former aid minister who resigned in 2017 over undisclosed meetings with Israeli officials, and employment minister Alok Sharma.

More women are also expected to serve as full Cabinet members. 20

Two junior ministers have already quit over Johnson's plans, and Chancellor Philip Hammond and justice minister David Gauke have both said they plan to resign before they are sacked.

In one of his first appointments before moving into Downing Street, Johnson poached senior Sky boss Andrew Griffith as his business adviser, tasked with 25 repairing relations with the corporate sector ahead of Brexit.

Johnson has pledged to negotiate a new divorce deal with the EU to secure a smooth transition. But if the bloc continues to refuse to renegotiate, he has promised to leave anyway — "do or die" — on the current agreed date of Oct. 31, Halloween.

— Based on a report on Reuters.com —

〈ニュース解説〉 "Brexit（英国の EU からの離脱）" に関する EU との交渉に行き詰まったティリーザ・メイ首相は、2019 年 5 月辞意を表明。その後任となる与党保守党の党首選挙で、ボリス・ジョンソン氏が勝利した。同氏は、EU 離脱を主唱してきた強硬派。離脱の是非を問う国民投票の責任を取って、当時のキャメロン首相が辞任した際も、首相候補の下馬評に上がったが、離脱現実化に対する内外のショックの大きさに尻込みし、辞退したとされる。新政権は、EU との「合意なき離脱」も辞さない覚悟だったが、その後の議会運営は困難に遭遇することとなった。

(Notes)

◆ **Stepping into power, Johnson seeks more diverse Cabinet** 「ジョンソン政権始動　より多様な内閣（閣僚登用）を目指す」（"step into" は「〜を始める、取り掛かる」の意。"power" は首相職及び政権を指す。"diverse cabinet" は、性別、出自、人種等が従来よりも多様な内閣）

◆ (L. 1) **Boris Johnson** ボリス・ジョンソン（米国生まれ。イートン校、オックスフォード大学を経て、英紙デイリー・テレグラフの記者となり、EU（欧州連合）に批判的な記事を書く。後に政界入りし、下院議員、ロンドン市長を経て、メイ政権の外相となったが、穏健な離脱案に反対して辞任。後任外相のジェレミー・ハント氏との保守党党首選の決戦投票を制し、第 77 代首相となる。特徴のある容姿、過激な言動により保守党の異端児とされてきたが、国民的な人気があり、親しみを持って「ボリス」と呼ばれる。親米派）

◆ (L. 2) **top team in a government** 内閣（"cabinet" の言い換え。同語の繰返しを避ける英語用法）

◆ (L. 2-3) **delivering Brexit by the end of October, with or without a deal** （EU との）合意の有無にかかわらず 10 月末までに離脱を達成する［EU との合意で、2019 年 10 月 31 日が "Brexit" 実行の最終期限となっていた。英国・北アイルランドと陸上で接するアイルランド共和国との間に物理的国境を設けないことの "backstop（安全策）" として、当面、英国が EU との関税同盟に残る代替策がメイ政権と EU で合意されたが、英議会は拒否。英 EU 間の通関のあり方も含めた合意ができないと、離脱後、両地域で物流の停滞等の大混乱が予想されていた］

◆ (L. 4) **the former London mayor** 前ロンドン市長（ジョンソン氏を指す）

◆ (L. 4) **Theresa May** ティリーザ・メイ前首相（「テリーザ」との表記もあるが英国人の発音は「ティリーザ」に近い）

◆ (L. 5) **the Conservative Party** 英国保守党（"the Tory" の別称がある）

◆ (L. 5-6) **the United Kingdom** 連合王国［正式名称「グレート・ブリテン及び北アイルランド連合王国（the United Kingdom of Great Britain and Northern Ireland）」から。略称 "the UK"］

◆ (L. 5-6) **campaign that put 〜 showdown with the European Union** 英国として欧州連合と（強硬離脱も辞さない）最終対決を行うことを争点とする選挙戦（後出 "the bloc" も EU を指す）

◆ (L. 7-8) **the world's fifth-largest economy** 世界第 5 位の経済（英国及び英国経済を指す）

◆ (L. 8) **divorce from the EU** 欧州連合からの離脱（"divorce" はもともと「離婚」の意）

◆ (L. 12) **Downing Street** ダウニング街（同 10 番地の首相官邸を指す。隣地の 11 番地は財務相官邸）

◆ (L. 12-13) **hand in her resignation to the Queen** （エリザベス）女王に辞表を提出する

◆ (L. 14) **the pound stuck 〜 against the U.S. dollar** 英ポンドは米ドルに対し過去 2 年間における最安値に近い水準で低迷した

◆ (L. 15) **"no-deal" Brexit** 「合意なき」離脱（英 EU 間が合意に達しないまま離脱を迎えること）

◆ (L. 16) **Chancellor, foreign secretary and Brexit minister** 財務相、外相及びブレグジット（離脱）担当相（"Chancellor" は英国財務相 "Chancellor of the Exchequer" の省略形）

◆ (L. 17) **ethnic minority politicians** 少数民族出身政治家

◆ (L. 18) **Priti Patel, the former aid minister** プリティ・パテル元国際開発大臣（インド系の保守党政治家。イスラエル閣僚との無断会合の責任を問われ大臣を辞任。反 EU 派）

◆ (L. 19) **employment minister Alok Sharma** アロク・シャルマ雇用大臣（インドのアグラ出身）

◆ (L. 20) **full Cabinet members** （閣内大臣等の）常勤閣僚［英国では、主に閣内大臣である上級大臣（senior minister）のほか閣内大臣を支援・補佐する閣外大臣である担当大臣、政務次官、政務官等からなる下級大臣（junior minister）がいる］

◆ (L. 22) **Philip Hammond** フィリップ・ハモンド（財務相）

◆ (L. 22) **justice minister David Gauke** デヴィッド・ゴーク司法大臣

◆ (L. 25) **senior Sky boss Andrew Griffith** スカイ（Sky）社の上級幹部アンドリュー・グリフィス氏［英国最大のメディア企業 Sky 社の最高執行責任者（COO：Chief Operating Officer）だったが、首相官邸の常勤顧問に就任した］

◆ (L. 27) **a new divorce deal** 新しい離脱協定

◆ (L. 29) **"do or die"** 断固として、いちかばちかで

ニュースを読んで、下記の設問に答えよ。

---

1. 本文の内容と一致するものには T (True) を、一致しないものには F (False) を記せ。

(   ) (1) The newly appointed British prime minister, Boris Johnson, is expected to organise a more diverse Cabinet to grapple with not only Brexit but also the management of the UK economy.

(   ) (2) Theresa May is the successor to Boris Johnson as British prime minister.

(   ) (3) In response to the news of Mr Johnson's victory for the Tory leadership, the UK pound appreciated against the US dollar.

(   ) (4) Johnson's new Cabinet may consist of a number of ethnic minority politicians as well as of women.

(   ) (5) In support of Mr Johnson's political stance toward Brexit, two junior ministers have already resigned and some other ministers plan to do the same.

(   ) (6) Attaching great importance to a good relationship with the corporate sector, Mr Johnson recruited a senior executive of a media giant as a key liaison.

2. 次の英文を完成させるために、(a) ～ (d) から最も適切なものを 1 つ選べ。

Boris Johnson has expressed his strong determination to deliver Brexit on the current agreed date of Oct. 31,_____

   (a) if a new deal with the EU cannot be reached.

   (b) only if a new deal with the EU can be reached.

   (c) even if a new deal with the EU cannot be reached.

   (d) only if a new deal with the EU cannot be reached.

Natural
34
Slow
36

　　President Donald Trump said on Monday he will watch only "a little bit" of Robert Mueller's long-awaited (1) ＿＿＿＿＿＿＿＿＿＿＿＿＿＿＿＿＿ his 22-month inquiry into Russian interference in the 2016 US election and renewed his attacks on the former special counsel.

　　Mueller's (2) ＿＿＿＿＿＿＿＿＿＿＿＿＿＿＿＿＿ since the Justice Department released a redacted version of the former FBI director's report in April, as congressional Democrats struggle with whether to launch the impeachment process set out in the US Constitution (3) ＿＿＿＿＿＿＿＿＿＿＿＿＿＿＿＿＿ .

Natural
35
Slow
37

　　Mueller's report said the investigation found insufficient evidence to prove that Trump and his campaign engaged in a criminal conspiracy with Russia despite the numerous contacts. The report did not reach a conclusion on whether Trump (4) ＿＿＿＿＿＿＿＿＿＿＿＿＿＿＿＿＿ but did not exonerate him.

　　Trump has attacked the Mueller investigation and the FBI inquiry that Preceded it (5) ＿＿＿＿＿＿＿＿＿＿＿＿＿＿＿＿＿ and repeated the words "No Collusion! No obstruction!" in Twitter posts even though Mueller did not come to either conclusion.

— Based on a report on Reuters.com —

〈ニュース解説〉　2016年の米大統領選では、ロシア政府が情報操作によりトランプ氏に有利な工作を行ったとされる。その真相と、トランプ氏側の関与について捜査した報告書が出されたが、同大統領の任命したウィリアム・バー司法長官は報告書の編集版を提出、大統領の無実を断言したため、議会側は事実を明らかにすべきとして、前特別検査官の議会証言を要求、これを実現させた。2020年大統領選をにらみ、トランプ弾劾に結び付けたい民主党と、関与を否定する大統領とのせめぎあいが続く。

(Notes)

Robert Mueller ロバート・モラー　**Russian interference in the 2016 US election** 2016年米大統領選におけるロシアの干渉疑惑　**the former special counsel** 前特別検察官（モラー氏を指す）　**Justice Department** 米司法省　**redacted version** 編集版（文字に色塗り等を加えて作成した要約版）　**the former FBI director** 元連邦捜査局長官（モラー氏を指す。同氏の特別検察官就任前の役職）　**congressional Democrats** 米議会民主党　**impeachment process**（大統領）弾劾手続　**the US Constitution** アメリカ合衆国憲法　**insufficient evidence** 不十分な証拠　**criminal conspiracy** 共同謀議（罪）（後出の "collusion" も同義）　**exonerate** 潔白だとする　**"No Collusion! No obstruction!"** 共謀もなければ、司法妨害もなかった！

■問A 米国政府関連用語 (a) ～ (i) にそれぞれ入るべき1語を下記の語群から選びその番号を記せ。

司法省	→	Department of (a)
財務省	→	Department of the (b)
内務省	→	Department of the (c)
国防総省	→	Department of (d)
中央情報局	→	Central (e) Agency
国家安全保障会議	→	National (f) Council
連邦捜査局	→	Federal Bureau of (g)
米国通商代表部	→	Office of the United States (h) Representative
国土安全保障省	→	Department of (i) Security

1. Defense   2. Homeland   3. Intelligence   4. Interior   5. Investigation
6. Justice   7. Security   8. Trade   9. Treasury

■問B (a) ～ (o) にそれぞれ対応する英文名称を下記の語群から選びその番号を記せ。

(a) （米）連邦議会　　　(b) （米）下院　　　　(c) （米）上院
(d) （英）議会　　　　　(e) （英）下院　　　　(f) （英）上院
(g) （米）民主党　　　　(h) （米）共和党　　　(i) （英）自由民主党
(j) （英）労働党　　　　(k) （英）保守党　　　(l) （米）国務長官
(m) （米）司法長官　　　(n) （英）内相　　　　(o) （英）財務相（蔵相）

1. Attorney General   2. Chancellor of the Exchequer
3. Congress   4. Conservative Party
5. Democratic Party   6. Home Secretary
7. House of Commons   8. House of Lords
9. House of Representatives   10. Labour Party
11. Liberal Democratic Party   12. Parliament
13. Republican Party   14. Secretary of State
15. Senate

■問C (a) ～ (e) のアジア関連用語をそれぞれ和訳せよ。

(a) National People's Congress

(b) People's Liberation Army

(c) People's Daily

(d) Republic of Korea (ROK)

(e) Democratic People's Republic of Korea (DPRK)

The world of features ― フィーチャー・ニュースの世界

"feature news"（フィーチャー・ニュース）は日本語では「特集記事」や「読み物」などと訳される。また、"hard news" と対比して "soft news" と呼ばれることもある。日本を台風が直撃し、その当日あるいは翌日、その被害を報じれば "hard news" である。その後、台風で家を失った住民の生活に焦点を当てて報じれば "feature news" となる。新聞などで報じられるニュースの大半は "hard news" であるが、報道のスピードという点で新聞はインターネットに遅れを取らざるを得ず、インターネットの普及に伴い、新聞の記事に占める "feature news" の割合が増加傾向にあるとの指摘もある。

このトピックを英文で読んでみよう。

Some old-timers treat news and features as if they're two separate things. News, they insist, is the factual reporting of serious events, while features involve all that other, nonessential stuff. It's not that simple, though. Journalists often find it difficult to distinguish between news and features. News stories usually focus on events that are timely and public: government activity, crime, disasters. Feature stories often focus on issues that are less timely and more personal: trends, relationships, entertainment. News stories tell you what happened; feature stories offer you advice, explore ideas and make you laugh and cry.

NEWS MEDIA IN THE WORLD

通信社　News Agencies (2)

✔　世界最初の近代的通信社は 1835 年フランスに生まれたアバスを母体とする AFP 通信（Agence France-Presse）。19 世紀半ばに創立の英国のロイター通信（Reuters）も業界の老舗。同時期に米国で設立された AP 通信（Associated Press）は組合型通信社の最大手。両社とも全世界に取材網を持ち、近時は経済ニュースにも力を入れる。経済情報の分野では Bloomberg の影響力も侮れない。

NEWS 7

Disk 1
38

Japan's Naruhito in 1st speech vows to stay close to people

Japan's new Emperor Naruhito inherited Imperial regalia and seals as proof of his succession and pledged in his first public address Wednesday to follow his father's example in devoting himself to peace and staying close to the people.

Naruhito succeeded to the Chrysanthemum Throne at midnight after Akihito abdicated.   5

"When I think about the important responsibility I have assumed, I am filled with a sense of solemnity," he said. Naruhito noted that his father was devoted to praying for peace and sharing joys and sorrows of the people, while showing compassion.

He said he will "reflect deeply" on the path trodden by Akihito and past emperors,   10
and promised to abide by the Constitution to fulfill his responsibility as a national symbol while "always turning my thoughts to the people and standing with them."

"I sincerely pray for the happiness of the people and the further development of the nation as well as the peace of the world," he said.

His wife and daughter, Empress Masako and 17-year-old Princess Aiko, were   15
barred from the ceremony, where only adult male royals participated. Only his brother, now Crown Prince Fumihito, and his uncle Prince Hitachi were allowed to witness. Their guests included a female Cabinet minister, however, as the Imperial House Law has no provision on the gender of the commoners in attendance.

Japan was in a festive mood celebrating an imperial succession that occurred   20
by retirement rather than by death. Many people stood outside the palace Tuesday to reminisce about Akihito's era, others joined midnight events when the transition occurred, and more came to celebrate the beginning of Naruhito's reign.

The emperor under Japan's constitution is a symbol without political power. Naruhito is free of influence from Japan's imperial worship that was fanned by the   25
wartime militarist government that had deified the emperor as a living god until his grandfather renounced that status after Japan's 1945 war defeat.

In an annual news conference marking his Feb. 23 birthday, Naruhito said he was open to taking up a new role that "suits the times." But he said his father's work will be his guidepost.   30

— *Based on an AP report on VOANews.com* —

〈ニュース解説〉　2019年5月1日、新天皇の即位と共に「令和」の時代が始まった。天皇は終身在位が原則となっているが、前天皇が高齢となったことにより一代限りの退位を認める退位特例法が成立、生前退位での皇位継承となった。平成時代、常に国民に寄り添う姿勢を示し続けた前天皇・皇后陛下の姿に皇室への支持は大きく広がったとされており、新たな時代への期待に日本は祝賀ムードに包まれた。

(Notes)

◆ **Naruhito** （徳仁）天皇陛下［第126代天皇。59歳での即位は記録が残る8世紀以降では2番目に高齢での皇位継承。日本では通常、報道も含め、天皇や皇太子、宮家本人は名前を呼ばない。在位にある天皇は「天皇陛下」又は「今上（きんじょう）陛下」と呼ぶ］

◆ (L. 1)　**Imperial regalia and seals**　［"Imperial regalia" は「皇位のしるし」の意で、ここでは「剣璽等承継の儀（けんじとうしょうけいのぎ）」で即位の証として継承される「三種の神器」を指す。三種の神器とは剣・玉・鏡のことで、剣璽とはその中の剣と玉を意味する。"seal" は「印章」の意で、ここでは国事行為の際に使用される国璽（こくじ）と御璽（ぎょじ）を指す。国璽は外交文書や国家の重要文書に押される国家の象徴としての印章であり、御璽は「天皇御璽」の印字を有する天皇の印章］

◆ (L. 2)　**his first public address**　［「剣璽等承継の儀」の後に行われた「即位後朝見の儀（そくいごちょうけんのぎ）」で天皇陛下が即位後初めて述べられた「おことば」を指す。即位後朝見の儀は、天皇陛下が即位された後、三権の長、閣僚、都道府県知事など、国民の代表に初めて公式に会われる儀式。剣璽等承継の儀では参列が許されなかった女性皇族も即位後朝見の儀には参列された］

◆ (L. 4)　**Chrysanthemum Throne**　皇位（News4　Notes 参照）

◆ (L. 4)　**Akihito**　（明仁）前天皇　［現在の称号は「上皇（Emperor Emeritus）」。在位は1989年1月7日から2019年4月30日。平成31年、85歳での退位となった］

◆ (L. 15)　**Empress Masako and 17-year-old Princess Aiko**　（雅子）皇后陛下と愛子内親王殿下（17）

◆ (L. 17)　**Crown Prince Fumihito**　秋篠宮（文仁）皇嗣殿下［「皇嗣（こうし）」は皇位継承順位第1位の皇族を指す呼称であるため、英語表記は「皇太子」と同じ "Crown Prince"。皇位継承順位第2位は秋篠宮家の長男悠仁（ひさひと）親王殿下］

◆ (L. 17)　**Prince Hitachi**　常陸宮（正仁）（ひたちのみやまさひと）殿下（上皇陛下の弟で、継承順位は第3位）

◆ (L. 18)　**Cabinet minister**　閣僚

◆ (L. 18-19)　**Imperial House Law**　皇室典範（皇位継承や摂政など、皇室に関する重要事項を定めた法律）

◆ (L. 19)　**commoner**　一般人

◆ (L. 22)　**reminisce about**　〜を回想する、思い出を語る

◆ (L. 26)　**deify the emperor as a living god**　天皇を「現人神（あらひとがみ）」として神格化する（「現人神」は「人の姿をした神」の意。第二次世界大戦終結まで天皇を指す言葉として用いられた）

1. 本文の内容と一致するものには T (True) を、一致しないものには F (False) を記せ。

(1) 　(　　) The new Emperor Naruhito ascended the Chrysanthemum Throne, followed by his father's abdication.

(2) 　(　　) In his first speech, the new emperor paid tribute to former Emperor Akihito, pledging to follow in his footsteps.

(3) 　(　　) No female members were allowed to attend the inheritance ritual, including Empress Masako and guests.

(4) 　(　　) Many people gathered to mourn the end of the Heisei era rather than celebrating a new era.

(5) 　(　　) The emperor is barred from exercising political power, but serves as a national symbol.

2. 日本国憲法第 1 章は全 8 条から成り、天皇及び皇室について定めている。以下は日本国憲法第 1 章の第 1 条、第 2 条及びその英訳であるが、空所に入るべき適語を語群から選んで完成せよ。

第 1 条
「天皇は、日本国の象徴であり日本国民統合の象徴であって、この地位は、主権の存する日本国民の総意に基づく」

Article 1.
The Emperor shall be the (1. 　　　　　　) of the State and of the (2. 　　　　　　) of the people, deriving his position from the (3. 　　　　　　) of the people with whom resides sovereign power.

第 2 条
「皇位は、世襲のものであって、国会の議決した皇室典範の定めるところにより、これを継承する」

Article 2.
The Imperial Throne shall be (4. 　　　　　　) and succeeded to in accordance with the Imperial House Law passed by the (5. 　　　　　　).

Cabinet, credentials, Diet, dynastic, honors, symbol, right, unity, will

音声を聞き、下線部を補え。（2回録音されています。1回目はナチュラルスピード、2回目はスロースピードです。）

Natural 40
Slow 42

About 613,000 people aged 40 to 64 are believed to fall into the category of recluses, (1) _____ without working, the government's first survey on the age group showed Friday.

The estimated number of recluses, known as *hikikomori*, in that age group is (2) _____. There are an estimated 541,000 recluses that fall into the younger age bracket, a Cabinet Office survey in 2015 showed. The total number of social recluses in Japan is thought to be over 1 million.

Natural 41
Slow 43

The Health, Labor and Welfare Ministry defines *hikikomori* as people who have remained isolated at home (3) _____, not going to school or work and not interacting with people outside their family.

One in three *hikikomori* aged between 40 and 44 — (4) _____ an "employment ice age" when new graduates found it hard to secure jobs — became socially reclusive between the ages of 20 and 24 years old, suggesting their inability to find work was behind the problem (5) _____.

— *Based on a report on Japantimes.com* —

〈ニュース解説〉　中高年のひきこもりに関する全国規模の調査が初めて実施され、中高年のひきこもり総数が若年層を上回る結果が出た。これまで若年層の問題と考えられてきたひきこもりの問題が高年齢化している実態が明らかになり、今後、新たな支援が社会の課題となっている。

(Notes)
recluse（本来は「隠遁者、世捨て人」の意だが、ここでは「ひきこもり」の意で用いられている）　**bracket** 区分、層　**Cabinet Office survey** 内閣府の調査　**Health, Labor and Welfare Ministry** 厚生労働省（正式名称は "Ministry of Health, Labour and Welfare" と Labour が英国式綴り）　**"employment ice age"**「就職氷河期」　**reclusive** 社会から隔離された

■問A　空所 (a) ～ (j) にそれぞれ入るべき 1 語を下記の語群から選びその番号を記せ。

体罰	→	(a) punishment
帰国子女	→	(b) children
ひきこもり	→	social (c)
ネットいじめ	→	online (d)
学級崩壊	→	classroom (e)
適応障害	→	(f) disorder
性同一性障害	→	(g) identity disorder
核家族	→	(h) family
育児休暇	→	maternity (i)
共働き世帯	→	(j)-earner household

1. adjustment	2. bullying	3. corporal	4. disintegration
5. dual	6. gender	7. leave	8. nuclear
9. returnee	10. withdrawal		

■問B　(a) ～ (i) にそれぞれ対応する英語表現を下記の語群から選びその番号を記せ。

(a) 不登校	(b) 停学	(c) 過食症
(d) 拒食症	(e) 認知症	(f) 養子縁組
(g) 一神教	(h) 多神教	(i) 無神論

1. adoption	2. anorexia	3. atheism
4. bulimia	5. dementia	6. monotheism
7. polytheism	8. suspension	9. truancy

■問C　空所 (a) ～ (c) にそれぞれ入るべき 1 語を下記の語群から選びその番号を記せ。

人間国宝	→	living national (a)
世界文化遺産	→	world cultural (b)
文化勲章	→	(c) of Culture

1. heritage	2. Order	3. treasure

THE WORLD OF ENGLISH JOURNALISM

From print to the web ― 紙媒体からウェブの重層的構造へ

新聞協会の調査によると、日本における日刊紙発行部数（一般紙とスポーツ紙の双方を含む。朝刊・夕刊セットは1部と計上）は1999年の約5,376万部から2010年には約4,932万部へと減少傾向にある。今後新聞などの紙媒体が消滅してしまうことはないだろうが、ウェブ・ニュース（オンライン・ニュース）には、新聞にはない魅力がある。すなわち、ウェブ・ニュースは様々なメディアの融合体で、新聞のようにニュースを横並びに読むのではなく、ワン・クリックで様々なメディアや情報に重層的にアクセスすることができる。

このトピックを英文で読んでみよう。

Print journalism won't go extinct. But it'll become increasingly difficult to compete against the allure of digital media, where editors can combine text, photos, audio, video, animated graphics, interactive chat and much more. Online media offer readers more variety. Stories, images and digital extras can be linked together in layers, with related options just a click away. Instead of arranging stories side by side, the way traditional newspapers do, online news sites link related topics in layers that allow readers to roam from story to story.

NEWS MEDIA IN THE WORLD

通信社　News Agencies (3)

✓ ロシア国営のイタル・タス通信（ITAR-TASS）は、ソビエト連邦時代の1925年に誕生したタス通信（TASS）が母体。冷戦期は、政府の公式情報発信機関だったが、ソビエト崩壊後、規模を縮小。中国の新華社通信 "Xinhua News Agency" も国営で中国政府及び共産党の公式見解を報道。政治問題などについて、報道内容や時間的対応状況から、政府の意向や内部事情などを占うことも多い。

NEWS 8

TV celebrities and coaches charged in college bribery scheme

Disk 2

BOSTON — Fifty people, including Hollywood stars Felicity Huffman and Lori Loughlin, were charged Tuesday in a scheme in which wealthy parents allegedly bribed college coaches and other insiders to get their children into some of the nation's most selective schools.

Federal authorities called it the biggest college admissions scam ever prosecuted 5 by the U.S. Justice Department, with the parents accused of paying an estimated $25 million in bribes.

At least nine athletic coaches and 33 parents, many of them prominent in law, finance, fashion, the food and beverage industry and other fields, were charged.

The coaches worked at such schools as Yale, Stanford, Georgetown, Wake 10 Forest, the University of Texas, the University of Southern California, and the University of California at Los Angeles.

No students were charged, with authorities saying that in many cases the teenagers were unaware of what was going on. Several of the colleges involved made no mention of taking any action against the students. 15

The scandal is certain to inflame longstanding complaints that children of the wealthy and well-connected have the inside track in college admissions — sometimes through big, timely donations from their parents — and that privilege begets privilege.

The central figure in the scheme was identified as admissions consultant William Singer, founder of the Edge College & Career Network of Newport Beach, California. 20

Prosecutors said that parents paid Singer big money from 2011 through last month to bribe coaches and administrators to falsely make their children look like star athletes to boost their chances of getting accepted. The consultant also hired ringers to take college entrance exams for students, and paid off insiders at testing centers to correct students' answers. 25

Some parents spent hundreds of thousands of dollars and some as much as $6.5 million to guarantee their children's admission, officials said.

Authorities said coaches in such sports as soccer, sailing, tennis, water polo and volleyball took payoffs to put students on lists of recruited athletes, regardless of their ability or experience. Once they were accepted, many of these students didn't 30 play the sports in which they supposedly excelled.

Mark Sklarow, an independent education consultant unconnected to the case, said the scandal "certainly speaks to the fact that the admissions process is broken."

"It's so fraught with anxiety, especially at the elite schools," he said, "that I think it can't be surprising that millionaires who have probably never said no to their kids 35 are trying to play the system in order to get their child accepted."

— Based on a report on AP News —

〈ニュース解説〉 米国の名門大学数校を巻きこんだ過去最大規模の不正入学事件では、富裕層の親たちが子供を名門大学に入学させるため、大学関係者に多額の賄賂を渡していた事実が明らかになった。支払ったとされる賄賂の総額はおよそ 28 億円。米国の大学の入学制度は多額の寄付金を出す富裕層に有利である実態は以前から問題視されていたが、今回の事件はそういった合法的な「正規ルート」ではなく、完全な不正行為により入学が優遇されていた。

(Notes)

◆ **TV celebrities and coaches charged in college bribery scheme** 「（米）大学不正入学で TV 俳優や運動部コーチらを起訴」（ヘッドラインでは簡潔化のために be 動詞がしばしば省略される。ここでは受動態 "were charged" の "were" が省略されている）

◆ (L. 1) **Felicity Huffman** フェリシティ・ハフマン［米女優。2004 年から 2012 年に放送された TV ドラマ「デスパレートな妻たち（"Desperate Housewives"）」に主人公の 1 人として出演し、2005 年公開の映画「トランスアメリカ（"Transamerica"）」では、アカデミー賞主演女優賞にノミネートされた］

◆ (L. 1-2) **Lori Loughlin** ロリ・ロックリン（米女優。1987 年から 1995 年に放送されたシチュエーションコメディ「フルハウス（"Full House"）」に出演）

◆ (L. 2) **allegedly** 申し立てによると、真偽のほどは不明だが

◆ (L. 3) **bribe** 〜に賄賂を贈る（L.7 の bribe は名詞で「賄賂」）

◆ (L. 6) **U.S. Justice Department** 米司法省

◆ (L. 10-12) **Yale, Stanford, Georgetown, Wake Forest, the University of Texas, the University of Southern California, and the University of California at Los Angeles** イェール大学、スタンフォード大学、ジョージタウン大学、ウェイク・フォレスト大学、テキサス大学、南カリフォルニア大学、及びカリフォルニア大学ロサンゼルス校（UCLA）（これらはすべて全米屈指の名門大学）

◆ (L. 15) **take action against** 〜に対処する、措置を講じる

◆ (L. 17) **well-connected** （親戚・知人などに）良い縁故のある、有力なコネを持った

◆ (L. 17) **inside track** （本来は「陸上競技用トラックのインコース、最も内側のコース」の意だが、転じて「（競争相手よりも）有利な立場」という意味で用いられている）

◆ (L. 19) **central figure** 中心人物、首謀者

◆ (L. 19-20) **admissions consultant William Singer, founder of the Edge College & Career Network of Newport Beach, California** カリフォルニア州ニューポートビーチにある「エッジ・カレッジ＆キャリアネットワーク」の設立者兼入学コンサルタントのウィリアム・シンガー（被告）（ニューポートビーチは全米でも有数の高級住宅街。シンガー被告は進学指導会社と銘打って裏口入学を斡旋・仲介していた）

◆ (L. 24) **ringer** 替え玉

◆ (L. 24) **college entrance exams** 大学入学試験［全米共通の大学進学適性試験 "SAT（Scholastic Assessment Test）" や "ACT（The American College Testing Program）" などのこと］

◆ (L. 24) **pay off** 〜に賄賂を贈る（L.29"took payoffs" の "payoff" は名詞で「賄賂」）

◆ (L. 29) **lists of recruited athletes** スポーツ推薦枠のリスト（米国の大学では、運動部が献金集めや知名度アップに大きく貢献するため、優秀な選手を集めることに力を入れている）

◆ (L. 32) **Mark Sklarow, an independent education consultant** 独立系教育コンサルタントのマーク・スクラロー氏

◆ (L. 33) **speak to** 〜を証明する、〜の証拠となる

◆ (L. 34) **It's so fraught with anxiety, …that I think…** （"it" は前の文章の "the admissions process" を指す。"anxiety" は「受験生やその親が抱いている不安感」の意。ここは so…that 構文となっている）

◆ (L. 36) **play the system** 制度を巧みに利用する

ニュースを読んで、下記の設問に答えよ。

1. 本文の内容と一致するものには T (True) を、一致しないものには F (False) を記せ。

(   ) (1) When this scam was revealed, all the students involved in the case were accused of cheating in admissions tests.

(   ) (2) William Singer used various illegal tactics to get the children of the wealthy parents into prestigious schools.

(   ) (3) When those children were not qualified for admission into some of the most selective schools, fake athletic credentials were created.

(   ) (4) The students admitted on fake athletic credentials were forced to play the sport after entering universities.

(   ) (5) Mr. Sklarow expressed surprise at the alleged scandal, because the US college admission system should not be biased in favor of wealthy people.

2. 本文で、William Singer 被告が行ったと記述されていないものは次のうちどれか。
(a) ～ (e) から一つ選び記号で答えよ。

(a) to organize bribes for cheating on college entrance exams

(b) to use connections with coaches at elite schools

(c) to make someone take the test for the students

(d) to make someone fix the answers on the tests

(e) to recruit athletic students who are capable team leaders

音声を聞き、下線部を補え。（2回録音されています。1回目はナチュラルスピード、2回目はスロースピードです。）

Natural 3
Slow 5

A major fire has engulfed the medieval cathedral of Notre-Dame in Paris,
(1) _____ .

The 850-year-old Gothic building's spire and roof have collapsed but the main structure, including the two bell towers, has been saved, officials say.

Firefighters are still working to contain the blaze as teams try to (2) _____   5
_____ .

President Emmanuel Macron called it a "terrible tragedy." The cause of the fire is not yet clear.

Natural 4
Slow 6

Officials say (3) _____ that began after cracks appeared in the stone, sparking fears (4) _____   10
_____ .

Paris prosecutor's office said it had opened an inquiry into "accidental destruction by fire." A firefighter was seriously injured (5) _____ .

— Based on a report on BBC.com —

〈ニュース解説〉 パリ中心部にある世界的観光名所、ノートルダム大聖堂で大規模な火災が発生し、尖塔や屋根が焼失した。出火当時は閉館直後で観光客の被害はなかったが、完全に消火するまで8時間以上もかかり難航した。火災の原因は失火とみられている。同聖堂には火災報知機や消火器は設置されていたものの、スプリンクラーなどの設備が備えられておらず、火災に対する備えが脆弱であったことが大きな悲劇につながったとみられている。

(Notes)
engulf（炎などが）〜を飲み込む、巻き込む　**cathedral of Notre-Dame** ノートルダム大聖堂（「ノートルダム大聖堂」は "Notre Dame Cathedral" と表記されることも多い。「ノートルダム」はフランス語で「我々の貴婦人」の意で、聖母マリアを指す）　**Gothic** ゴシック様式の　**bell tower** 鐘楼（同大聖堂正面の南北の塔を指す）　**President Emmanuel Macron** エマニュエル・マクロン大統領　**open an inquiry into** 〜の取り調べを始める

■問A 空所 (a) ～ (k) にそれぞれ入るべき1語を下記の語群から選びその番号を記せ。

業務上過失	→	professional (a)
脱税	→	tax (b)
著作権侵害	→	copyright (c)
フィッシング詐欺	→	(d) scam
おとり捜査	→	(e) operation
捜査令状	→	search (f)
物的証拠	→	(g) evidence
状況証拠	→	(h) evidence
精神鑑定	→	(i) test
冤罪	→	(j) charge
自宅軟禁	→	house (k)

1. arrest　　2. circumstantial　　3. dodge　　4. false
5. negligence　　6. phishing　　7. physical　　8. piracy
9. psychiatric　　10. sting　　11. warrant

■問B (a) ～ (q) にそれぞれ対応する英語表現を下記の語群から選びその番号を記せ。

(a) 重罪　(b) 軽犯罪　(c) 違反　(d) 名誉棄損
(e) 拘留　(f) 窃盗　(g) 万引き　(h) スパイ行為
(i) 贈収賄　(j) 監禁　(k) 襲撃　(l) 自白
(m) 大量殺人　(n) 残虐行為　(o) 銃撃　(p) 刺傷
(q) 脱走者

1. assault　　2. atrocity　　3. bribery　　4. confession
5. confinement　　6. custody　　7. defamation　　8. espionage
9. felony　　10. fugitive　　11. massacre　　12. misdemeanor
13. offense　　14. shooting　　15. shoplifting　　16. stabbing
17. theft

■問C (a) ～ (h) をそれぞれ和訳せよ。

(a) abuse　　(b) charge　　(c) corruption
(d) fraud　　(e) interrogation　　(f) ransom
(g) robbery　　(h) smuggling

Broadcast news — 放送ニュースの特質

放送ニュースは、テレビやラジオの映像や音声を通じて視聴者の感情に訴えることができ、現実を生で伝える力がある。視聴者も面倒な記事を読む煩わしさから解放され、頭を使うことが少なくて済むから大人気。新聞や雑誌といった紙媒体のようなニュースの深みや掘り下げはないが、視聴者へのアピール度や即時性（immediacy）といった面では軍配が上がる。なお、最近では従来のテレビやラジオに加えて、インターネットで聴けるネット・ラジオ、携帯音楽プレイヤーに音声データ・ファイルとして配信される "Podcast"（ポッドキャスト）や携帯電話で視聴できる "One-Seg television"（ワンセグ・テレビ）等、放送ニュースのメディアも実に多様化してきている。

このトピックを英文で読んでみよう。

TV and radio journalism is neither better nor worse than print journalism. It's just different. Each form of media has strengths and weaknesses. Print journalism provides a level of depth, context and sheer information that television and radio newscasts can't supply. Broadcast journalism, through the power of dramatic video and engaging audio, offers emotional appeal, realism and immediacy that printed stories can't match. Watching or listening to a news broadcast generally requires less intellectual effort than reading a complex news story in a newspaper.

通信社　News Agencies (4)

✓ 日本の共同通信社（Kyodo News Service）と時事通信社（JIJI Press）は第 2 次大戦中の国策通信社・聯合通信が 1945 年に分割されて出来た、非営利の社団法人。中央、地方の新聞や放送へのニュース記事配信とともに、行政機関や民間会社への情報提供サービスを行っている。近時、アジアを中心に英語による国際的な発信活動にも力を入れている。

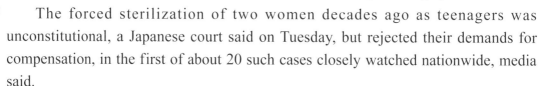

Chapter 9 　裁判・法令

NEWS 9

Court: Forced sterilizations unconstitutional, but no payout

Disk 2
7

The forced sterilization of two women decades ago as teenagers was unconstitutional, a Japanese court said on Tuesday, but rejected their demands for compensation, in the first of about 20 such cases closely watched nationwide, media said.

Tens of thousands of people were sterilized, many without their consent, under a ₅ government program aimed at preventing the birth of "inferior descendants" that ran until 1996.

Last month, Japan passed a law compensating the victims, many of whom were physically or cognitively disabled, while others suffered from mental illness or leprosy, now a curable disease, or simply grappled with behavioral problems. ₁₀

Tuesday's judgment, in the Sendai district court in northern Japan, was the first in a group of about 20 cases around the country suing the government for violations of human rights and demanding compensation.

8

One of the women is in her 60s and the other in her 70s, and they had demanded compensation of 71.5 million yen ($653,100), Japan Broadcasting Corp. (NHK) said. ₁₅

One of their lawyers told NHK that he was shocked by the compensation rejection, a view shared by one of the plaintiffs.

"We've been fighting this for 20 years, but this result has left me speechless," NHK quoted the older woman as saying.

Japan adopted the "Eugenics Protection Law" in 1948 as it struggled with food ₂₀ shortages and rebuilding a war-ravaged nation.

Before it was revoked, an estimated 25,000 people were sterilized, with at least 16,500 not having given consent to procedures a eugenics panel could approve, often after a cursory review. Few records remain.

Sterilizations peaked in the 1960s and 1970s, with the last surgery under the law ₂₅ dating to 1993.

— Based on a report on Reuters on asahi.com —

〈ニュース解説〉 旧優生保護法の下、障がいを理由に強制的に不妊手術を受けさせられたとして女性二人が国に損害賠償を求めた訴訟は、判決で国の行為は違憲であると認定されたものの、損害賠償請求は退けられた。手術から 20 年以上が経過したことで賠償請求権が消滅したとし、賠償制度の立法措置を設けてこなかった国の責任についても否定した。しかし、子を産み育てる可能性を奪い取られた同法の被害者たちはこれに納得しておらず、今後も国の責任を法廷で問い続けるとしている。

(Notes)

◆ **forced sterilization** 強制的な不妊手術、強制不妊

◆ **payout** （本来は「支払い金」の意だが、ここでは「損害賠償金」のこと）

◆ (L. 6) **government program** ［後出の "Eugenics Protection Law（優生保護法）" に基づく制度を指す。優生保護法は 1948 年から 1996 年まで長年にわたり存続し、優生思想を全国的に広く推し進めた。障がい者差別につながるとされた同法は 1996 年、「母体保護法」に改正され、強制的な不妊手術の規定が削除された］

◆ (L. 6) **"inferior descendants"** 「不良な子孫」

◆ (L. 8) **Japan passed a law compensating the victims** （2019 年 4 月に成立した「一時金支給法」のこと。旧優生保護法に基づき不妊手術を受けた被害者に一時金を支給することが法律で定められたが、「補償」との位置づけではなかったこと、金額も一律 320 万円で訴訟での請求額とは大きく隔たっていたことなどから被害者の反発を招いた）

◆ (L. 9) **leprosy** ハンセン病（らい菌によっておこる感染症で、らい病とも呼ばれた。毒性や感染力は非常に弱く現在は薬で完治する。しかし、かつては不治の病とされたため、国は強制隔離政策などを推進。ハンセン病患者は差別や偏見を受け、人権が著しく侵害された。国は、病態についての事実が解った後にも隔離政策を続け、法改正などの適切な措置を怠ったことの責任が問われた）

◆ (L. 11) **Sendai district court in northern Japan** 日本の北方（東北地方）にある仙台地裁（日本の地理に疎い読者に配慮して "northern Japan" と仙台の位置的情報を与えている。原告の二人は宮城県内に住む 60 代と 70 代の女性）

◆ (L. 15) **Japan Broadcasting Corp.(NHK)** 日本放送協会、NHK

◆ (L. 17) **plaintiff** 原告

◆ (L. 19) **quote someone as saying 〜** （人）が〜と述べたと報じる、伝える

◆ (L. 21) **war-ravaged** 戦争で荒廃した、戦争によって破壊された

◆ (L. 22) **revoke** 〜を廃止する、無効にする

◆ (L. 23) **eugenics panel** 優生保護委員会（優生手術を行うのに「適当」か否かを審査した委員会。医師の診断を経て申請を受けた場合に、優生保護法の規定要件を備えているかどうかを審査の上、手術の適否を決定し、手術対象者に通知することとなっていた）

◆ (L. 24) **cursory review** おざなりな調査

ニュースを読んで、下記の設問に答えよ。

1. 本文の内容と一致するものには T (True) を、一致しないものには F (False) を記せ。

(   ) (1) The Sendai district court dismissed a damage suit filed by two women, because the forced sterilization was constitutional.

(   ) (2) The purpose of the 1948 Eugenics Protection Law was to compensate the victims of forced sterilization.

(   ) (3) The Eugenics Protection Law deprived the victims of the right to have their own children.

(   ) (4) According to NHK, one of the plaintiffs expressed shock and anger over the court decision.

(   ) (5) About 25,000 people underwent sterilization with their consent.

2. 本文の訴訟では、子を産み育てるかどうかを自ら意思決定する「性と生殖に関する権利（リプロダクティブ・ライツ）」は幸福追求権などを規定した憲法 13 条に保証されているとして、「旧優生保護法は違憲」との判決が出された。以下は憲法 13 条及びその英訳であるが、空所に入るべき適語を語群から選んで完成せよ。

第十三条　すべて国民は、個人として尊重される。生命、自由及び幸福追求に対する国民の権利については、公共の福祉に反しない限り、立法その他の国政の上で、最大の尊重を必要とする。

Article 13.

All of the people shall be respected as ⁽¹⁾(   ). Their right to life, liberty, and the ⁽²⁾(   ) of happiness shall, to the ⁽³⁾(   ) that it does not interfere with the public ⁽⁴⁾(   ), be the ⁽⁵⁾(   ) consideration in ⁽⁶⁾(   ) and in other governmental affairs.

extent,   individuals,   legislation,   pursuit,   supreme,   welfare

音声を聞き、下線部を補え。（2回録音されています。1回目はナチュラルスピード、2回目はスロースピードです。）

Natural
9

Slow
11

  Japan's parliament enacted Wednesday a revised law banning parents and other guardians from physically punishing children following several fatal cases of abuse [(1)]   .

  Another law was also amended to strengthen the ability of child welfare centers to "intervene" in abuse cases by separating staff members in charge of taking children into protective custody from [(2)]   . 5

Natural
10

Slow
12

  Under the revised laws, local child consultation centers and related entities are urged to swiftly share information so that [(3)]   even if a child moves to a different area.

  Prefectural governments and child welfare centers are also urged to [(4)]   10
          , using medical and psychological expertise, to
[(5)]   .

— Based on a report on Kyodo News report —

〈ニュース解説〉「しつけ」と称した親の虐待で命を落とす子どもの被害が増え続けている。新たな悲劇が繰り返されることを防ぐため、2019年6月、児童福祉法などが改正された。体罰を法律で禁じている国は世界で54か国に及んでいるが、日本ではいまだに体罰容認の意識が根強く残っている。体罰禁止が法律に盛り込まれたことで、人々の意識や虐待防止体制が大きく進化すると期待されている。

(Notes)
child welfare center 児童相談所（L. 7 の "child consultation center" も同義）　**intervene** 介入する
protective custody 保護拘置（親の虐待から守るために一時的に子どもを保護すること）　**related entities** 関連機関

■問A　空所 (a) ～ (i) にそれぞれ入るべき 1 語を下記の語群から選びその番号を記せ。

陪審制度	→	(a) system
裁判員制度	→	(b) system
裁判長	→	(c) judge
国選弁護人	→	(d) lawyer
執行猶予付き判決	→	(e) sentence
終身刑	→	life (f)
死刑	→	death (g)
刑事訴訟	→	(h) action
民事訴訟	→	(i) action

1. civil	2. court-appointed	3. criminal	4. imprisonment
5. jury	6. lay judge	7. penalty	8. presiding
9. suspended			

■問B　(a) ～ (l) にそれぞれ対応する英語表現を下記の語群から選びその番号を記せ。

(a) 弁護士	(b) 検察官	(c) 原告
(d) 被告	(e) 裁判	(f) 起訴
(g) 証言	(h) 評決	(i) 判決
(j) 有罪判決	(k) 刑罰	(l) 恩赦

1. amnesty	2. conviction	3. defendant	4. judgment
5. lawyer	6. penalty	7. plaintiff	8. prosecution
9. prosecutor	10. testimony	11. trial	12. verdict

■問C　日本の司法制度に関係する (a) ～ (f) の用語をそれぞれ和訳せよ。

(a) Supreme Court

(b) high court

(c) district court

(d) family court

(e) summary court

(f) Supreme Public Prosecutors Office

THE WORLD OF ENGLISH JOURNALISM

Radio news reporting ― ラジオ・ニュースの難しさ

テレビのような映像がなく、新聞・雑誌のように長々と叙述できないのがラジオのニュース。ラジオの聞き手は何か他のことをしながらラジオ・ニュースを聞いている。そうなると、ニュースも簡潔、そして聞き手の注意を一発で喚起する書き方が要求される。記者には、ニュースを30秒でまとめる技術が求められる。"actuality" または "sound bite"（ニュースで繰り返し放送される録音テープからの抜粋）、"natural sound" または "ambient sound"（周囲の様子を伝えるような音声や環境音）、"lead-in"（ニュース番組の導入部分）等はラジオニュース関連の専門用語。テレビ・ニュースの用語と共通するものも多い。最近はインターネットで聞けるラジオサイトも増え、世界中のラジオ放送を無料で聞くことが出来る。ホームページでは豊富な英文記事の他に、ラジオ・ニュースも聴取できる。BBC World Service（英）、NPR（米）、ABC Radio National（豪）等にアクセスしてオンライン・ラジオ・ニュースを聴いてみよう。

このトピックを英文で読んでみよう。

Radio journalism may be the most challenging form of news reporting. You can't rely on graphics and images as TV reporters do. You can't write long, descriptive sentences and stories as print reporters do. When people are listening to your story on the radio, they're doing it while they dodge traffic, talk on their cell phone and do their makeup. So radio news writing needs to be as direct and attention-grabbing as possible. Word economy is the key. The best radio reporting is snappy yet eloquent, conversational yet concise, friendly yet authoritative. Most stories at most stations require their reporters to boil everything down to its 30-second essence.

NEWS 10

Disk 2
13

Japan to lead global push for ocean-friendly plastic

TOKYO---Japan looks to partner with the private sector to develop biodegradable plastic that causes little harm to the oceans, Nikkei has learned.

The proposal forms part of a campaign to rid the sea of plastic waste, and the overall plan will be presented Friday to cabinet members at Prime Minister Shinzo Abe's office.　　　　　　　　　　　　　　　　　　　　　　　　　　　　　　　　　5

Japan wants to focus on the burgeoning level of ocean plastic pollution during the Group of 20 gathering next month in Osaka. About 300 million tons of waste plastic are produced every year, the United Nations says, and estimates show that 8 million to 12 million tons end up in the oceans annually.

The Japanese plan calls for a public-private partnership to develop plastic　10 material that creates minimal environmental impact on the oceans. Such material might dissolve in seawater, for example. This undertaking would include fishing gear, given that a survey by an environmental group found that fishing nets make up 46 percent of the so-called Great Pacific Garbage Patch, which lies between Hawaii and California.　　　　　　　　　　　　　　　　　　　　　　　　　　　　　　15

14　　The government also intends to share the plastic plan with attendees of the Tokyo International Conference of African Development, set for late August in Yokohama.

This proposal goes in tandem with Tokyo's goal of recycling all plastic bottles.

The state will support installing recycling boxes beside vending machines, and　20 increase the frequency of collections. Pickup of plastic containers left on the ground will be conducted more often. Abe's government plans to offer incentives such as subsidies to get municipalities and other groups on board. Japan recycles plastic bottles at a greater percentage than in the United States or Europe.

Enforcement against pollution will grow stronger nationwide. Local　25 governments organize a week of patrols annually that search for illegal dumping, and the activity will be expanded. Japan will help emerging nations develop legal frameworks to combat plastic pollution, as well as train monitors in Southeast Asia.

— Based on a report on Nikkei Asian Review —

〈ニュース解説〉 日本は海洋プラスチック汚染問題解決を主導していくことを目指し、2050年までにはプラスチックごみによる新たな海洋汚染をゼロにする目標を掲げた「大阪ブルー・オーシャン・ビジョン」（"Osaka Blue Ocean Vison"）を2019年6月に大阪で開催されたG20首脳会議共同宣言に盛り込むことに成功した。プラスチックごみが海に流出すると波や日光で粉砕され、魚の体内に取り込まれ、そうした魚を食べた人間の健康をも害する可能性があると懸念されている。日本はプラスチックごみに対する一般市民の認識を高めていこうと、2020年の東京オリンピックの表彰台を廃棄プラスチックで作る予定。

(Notes)

◆ **Japan to lead global push for ocean-friendly plastic** 「日本主導で海洋環境に優しいプラスチックを世界的規模で推進へ」（英語ニュースの見出しでは「未来形」をこのように不定詞で表現することが多い）

◆ (L. 1-2) **biodegradable plastic** 生分解性プラスチック（自然界の微生物などにより水と二酸化炭素に分解されていく環境にやさしいプラスチック）

◆ (L. 4-5) **Prime Minister Shinzo Abe's office** 首相官邸（正式英語名称は Prime Minister's Office of Japan）

◆ (L. 7) **Group of 20 gathering next month in Osaka** （2019年6月28日、29日両日にわたり日本が初めて議長国を務めて行われたG20首脳会議。（Chapter4 Exercise2 参照）

◆ (L. 14) **Great Pacific Garbage Patch** 太平洋ごみベルト（北太平洋のハワイからカリフォルニアにかけて浮遊プラスチックなどの海洋ごみが集中している海域）

◆ (L. 17) **Tokyo International Conference of African Development** アフリカ開発会議
（略称 TICAD。1993年以降、日本が主導し、国連、国連開発会議、アフリカ連合委員会、世界銀行と共同で開催するアフリカ開発に関する国際会議。3年に1回の開催。第6回は2016年3月にスリランカのコロンボで、本記事にある第7回は横浜で開催）

◆ (L. 19) **Tokyo's goal** 政府目標（ここでは "Tokyo" は日本政府を意味する）

◆ (L. 19) **plastic bottle** ［ここではリサイクル可能なペット（PET）ボトルを指す。"PET" はボトルの素材として使われているポリエチレン・テレフタレート（polyethylene-terephthalate）の略。英語では「ピー・ティー・イー・」と発音する］

◆ (L. 28) **monitors** （ここではプラスチックごみの管理技術者を意味する）

ニュースを読んで、下記の設問に答えよ。

---

1. 本文の内容と一致するものには T (True) を、一致しないものには F (False) を記せ。

(   ) (1) Marine plastic pollution has been rapidly increasing.

(   ) (2) Most of the plastic waste produced in the world flows into oceans.

(   ) (3) The Great Pacific Garbage Patch extends from Japan to California

(   ) (4) Japan intends to cooperate with African countries to solve marine plastic pollution.

(   ) (5) Japan exceeds the US and Europe in terms of its plastic bottle recycling rate.

2. 下記は 2019 年の大阪 G20 で共同宣言に "Osaka Blue Ocean Vision" が盛り込まれたことを報じる記事の一部である。語群の語を正しく並べて下線部分を補充して英文を完成せよ。

The G20 leaders adopted the Osaka Blue Ocean Vision in the final statement, which _____to zero by 2050.

additional, commits, marine, plastic, reducing, to, waste

音声を聞き、下線部を補え。（２回録音されています。１回目はナチュラルスピード、２回目はスロースピードです。）

Natural
15

Slow
17

All medals at next summer's Olympics and Paralympics in Tokyo will be
(1) _____ , including discarded smartphones, digital
cameras and other handheld games and laptops, organizers revealed on Friday.

Officials said they (2) _____
by the end of March to extract the amount of gold, silver and bronze that will be   5
required to manufacture all the medals that will be awarded next year.

The organizing committee said municipal authorities had already collected
47,488 tons of junked devices by November, (3) _____
_____ with targets of 30.3kg of gold, 4,100kg of silver and 2,700kg of bronze.

Natural
16

Slow
18

The goal for bronze was reached in June, while more than 90 percent of the   10
gold and 85 percent of the silver has been collected, officials said.

"It is estimated that the remaining amounts of metal required to manufacture
all Olympic and Paralympic medals can be extracted from the devices already
donated."

The concept has been implemented in previous Olympics, most recently at   15
Rio 2016, where an estimated 30 percent of the silver and bronze medals were
wrought from recycled materials. But organizers noted the current project will
mark the first time (4) _____ with the donation
of consumer electronics.

— *Based on a report on gurdian.com* —

〈ニュース解説〉　東京オリンピック組織委員会は 2020 年東京オリンピック・パラリンピックのメダルを不要になった携帯電話や小型家電から作る「みんなのメダルプロジェクト」を 2017 年 4 月から 2019 年 3 月末まで実施した。必要なメダル 5000 個分の金、銀、銅がこのプロジェクトで集まった。携帯電話や小型家電には金、銀、銅等の貴金属が含まれているため、こうした廃棄家電から得られる資源は「都市鉱山」と呼ばれ、日本のように自国にこれといった鉱物資源を持たない国にとっては資源の安定供給を確保する一手段として注目されている。

(Notes)
organizers（東京オリンピック・パラリンピック組織委員会を指す。後出の "the organizing committee" も同委員会のこと）　**handheld games**（"handheld game consoles" を省略した表現。携帯型ゲーム機のこと）　**bronze** 銅（ブロンズ）［「ブロンズ」は「青銅」の意。銅（copper）にスズ（tin）を数パーセント混ぜた合金で、銅像やメダル、硬貨等に使われる。銅メダルは正確には青銅メダルとなるが、金、銀、銅という並びで慣例的に銅メダルと呼ぶ］　**Rio 2016**（2016 年にブラジルのリオデジャネイロで開催されたオリンピック・パラリンピック大会）

■問A　空所 (a) ～ (g) にそれぞれ入るべき 1 語を下記の語群から選びその番号を記せ。

光化学スモッグ　　　→　(a) smog

酸性雨　　　　　　　→　(b) rain

生物多様性　　　　　→　biological (c)

排ガス規制　　　　　→　(d) control

産業廃棄物　　　　　→　(e) waste

放射線廃棄物　　　　→　(f) waste

液化天然ガス　　　　→　(g) natural gas

1. acid	2. diversity	3. emission
4. industrial	5. liquefied	6. photochemical
7. radioactive		

■問B　(a) ～ (l) をそれぞれ和訳せよ。

(a) solar cell

(b) renewable energy

(c) geothermal power production

(d) wave-energy power station

(e) hydroelectric generation

(f) thermal power plant

(g) Nuclear Regulation Authority

(h) ecosystem

(i) ozone layer depletion

(j) environmentalist

(k) environmentally friendly

(l) pollutant

Media convergence ― メディアの融合化への流れ

昨今のジャーナリズムは、マルチメディアを駆使して情報を伝達する。1つのことを伝えるにも、写真、オーディオ、ビデオ（動画）、テキスト（文字データ）というようにあらゆる媒体を使って、より理想に近い情報を作り出し伝達することが出来るのがメディア融合の強みである。

このトピックを英文で読んでみよう。

Suppose you decided to profile Ludwig van Gogh, a brilliant painter and composer. Which medium, or media, would produce the best story? To display his paintings, you'd use photographs. To present his music, you'd use audio recordings. To show him at work—conducting an orchestra or painting—you'd use video footage. To explain the meaning and impact of his art, you'd use text. In short, to create the ideal profile, you'd need multimedia. Cross-platform journalism, media convergence—whatever you call it, it's an idea whose time has finally come.

NEWS MEDIA IN THE WORLD

新聞社 Newspapers (1)

✓ 英国では、高級紙と言われる *Daily Telegraph* や *Times*、*Guardian* などの他は、庶民を読者とするタブロイド判（tabloid）の大衆紙が多い。2015 年 7 月日本経済新聞社による買収の発表があった高級経済紙の *Financial Times*（略称 FT）は大判（broadsheet）でピンク色の用紙が特徴的。米国や欧州、アジアや日本で地域版を印刷発行する。欧州では、フランスの *Le Figaro*、*Le Monde*、ドイツの *Die Welt* なども有名。近年紙面の縮小が流行で *Guardian* や *Le Monde* など、大判とタブロイド判の中間の大きさのベルリナー判（Berliner format）を採用する新聞もある。*Times* もタブロイド判を発行している。

NEWS 11

Disk 2

(19) **By 2050, London's climate will be as warm as Barcelona's, says new study**

In 2050, London's climate will feel more like Barcelona's, according to a new climate change study.

If this sounds like a pleasant warming — think again. London could be facing severe drought, as Barcelona did in 2008, when it nearly ran out of drinking water and reservoirs ran close to dry. 5

Hundreds of other major cities worldwide could be facing droughts, flooding, storms, and other climate catastrophes, said the study, which was conducted by the Crowther Lab at ETH Zurich university.

Some of these climate effects aren't even known or predictable yet — a fifth of cities, including Kuala Lumpur, Jakarta, and Singapore, are facing conditions so 10 extreme they don't currently exist anywhere in the world, according to the study.

The study predicted the future climate conditions of 520 major cities worldwide, and paired those predictions with the conditions of cities today. By 2050, Madrid will feel more like Marrakesh, Seattle will feel like San Francisco, and New York will feel like Virginia Beach, according to the report. 15

(20) Drawing these city-to-city comparisons can "help people visualize the impact of climate change in their own city, within their lifetime," said Jean-Francois Bastin, lead author of the study.

An estimated 77 percent of cities around the world will see their climate conditions drastically change, indicating "the global scale of this climate change 20 threat and associated risks for human health," the study warned.

Regions with northern latitudes, including most of Europe, will face the most dramatic temperature changes — European cities are expected to become 3.5 degrees Celsius (6.3 Fahrenheit) warmer in the summer and 4.7 degrees Celsius (8.5 Fahrenheit) warmer in the winter, the study said. 25

In London, for example, the warmest month will rise by 5.9 degrees (10.6 Fahrenheit), leading to a mean annual temperature rise of 2.1 degrees (3.8 Fahrenheit).

These might not sound like significant shifts, but warming temperatures could encourage the spread of infectious disease, endanger food security, and lead to water shortages, said Alex Lo, a senior lecturer in climate change at the Victoria University 30 of Wellington in New Zealand.

— Based on a report on CNN.com —

〈ニュース解説〉 2019 年 7 月、世界気象機関（World Meteorological Organization, 略称 WMO）は、同年 6 月以降、北極圏で記録的高温となり山火事が多発した一方で、米国やバングラデシュでは洪水が起こるなど世界各地で様々な異常気象が出現していると発表した。同機関によると、同年 6 月のシベリアの平均気温は 1981 年から 2010 年の平均を約 10 度も上回った。近年こうした温暖化と異常気象の多発が懸念される中、スイス工科大学チューリッヒ校が発表した予測では、このままのペースで行くと 2050 年までに世界の主要都市は劇的に温暖化するとされている。

(Notes)

◆ **London** ロンドン（英国の首都、北緯 51 度）

◆ **Barcelona** バルセロナ（スペイン・カタルーニャ州の州都、北緯 41 度）

◆ (L. 8) **Crowther Lab at ETH Zurich university** スイス工科大学（ETH）チューリッヒ校クロウサー研究室（同校は、1855 年に設立され、科学技術・自然科学を対象とする世界有数の大学。ETH はドイツ語の校名の頭文字で、英語圏でもエー・テー・ハーと発音される。クロウサー研究室は、生態系研究を専門とする英国人若手科学者で同校教授のトーマス・クロウサーの研究室）

◆ (L. 10) **Kuala Lumpur, Jakarta, and Singapore** クアラルンプール、ジャカルタ及びシンガポール（前 2 都市はそれぞれ、マレーシア、インドネシアの首都。シンガポールは都市国家のため首都という概念はない）

◆ (L. 13) **Madrid** マドリッド（スペインの首都、北緯 40 度）

◆ (L. 14) **Marrakesh** マラケシュ（モロッコ南西部の都市、北緯 32 度）

◆ (L. 14) **Seattle** シアトル（米国ワシントン州北西部の都市、北緯 47 度）

◆ (L. 14) **San Francisco** サンフランシスコ（米国カリフォルニア州北部の都市、北緯 37 度）

◆ (L. 14) **New York** ニューヨーク（米国ニューヨーク州にある同国最大の都市、北緯 40 度）

◆ (L. 15) **Virginia Beach** バージニアビーチ（米国バージニア州南東端の都市、北緯 31 度）

◆ (L. 17) **Jean-Francois Bastin** ジャン・フランソワ・バスティン

◆ (L. 22) **regions with northern latitude** 北半球の地域、都市

◆ (L. 24) **Celsius** 摂氏（世界中で最も一般的に用いられている温度表示法。略称 "C"。これを提案したスウェーデンの天文学者の名に因むため、大文字で書き始められる。摂氏は "centigrade" とも表現される）

◆ (L. 24) **Fahrenheit** 華氏（米国の日常生活では現在でも広く使われている温度表示法。略称 "F"。これも提案したドイツの物理学者の名に因むため、大文字で書き始められる）

◆ (L. 30) **Alex Lo** アレックス・ロウ

◆ (L. 30) **senior lecturer** シニア・レクチャラー、上級講師［英国、オーストラリア、ニュージーランドの大学では教授（professor）の肩書きを持つ大学教員の数は日本と比べて少なく、シニア・レクチャラーやレクチャラーの肩書きの教員が多い］

◆ (L. 30-31) **Victoria University of Wellington** ビクトリア大学ウェリントン校（ニュージーランドの首都ウェリントンにある同校は同国で最も長い歴史を持つ）

　ニュースを読んで、下記の設問に答えよ。

1. 本文の内容と一致するものには T (True) を、一致しないものには F (False) を記せ。

(1)　(　) In 2008, London suffered a severe drought.

(2)　(　) According to a new study by a Swiss university, many big cities around the world could be affected by global climate change by 2050.

(3)　(　) European cities are expected to be over 5 degrees Celsius warmer both in the summer and the winter by 2050.

(4)　(　) By 2050, San Francisco's climate will be similar to that of Virginia Beach now.

(5)　(　) By 2050, the average annual temperature in London will rise more than 2 degrees Celsius from now.

2. 国連は 2019 年 6 月に発表した報告書の中で、気候変動が貧富の差による生活の著しい格差を生み出す「気候アパルトヘイト」現象が今後 10 年以内に出現する可能性があると警告している。下記はその警告について報道した CNN 記事の一部である。語群から適語を空所に補充して英文を完成させること。

Just last month, a new UN report warned that more than 120 million people could slip into ($^{1.}$　　　　　) within the next decade because of climate change, ($^{2.}$　　　　) a "climate apartheid" scenario where the ($^{3.}$　　　　) pay to ($^{4.}$　　　　) overheating, hunger and ($^{5.}$　　　　), while the ($^{6.}$　　　　) of the world is ($^{7.}$　　　　) to suffer.

(a)conflict,　(b)creating,　(c) escape,　(d)left,　(e)poverty,　(f)rest,　(g)wealthy

Natural
21
Slow
23

    Japanese seismologists believe that nearly 99 percent of their predictions related to massive earthquakes in the Pacific off central and western Japan are likely to be proven wrong, a survey conducted by Kansai University showed Sunday.

    While the government estimates there is a 70 to 80 percent chance of a magnitude 8-to-9 quake occurring along the Nankai Trough within the next 30 years, the survey underscores the difficulty of precisely predicting the [(1)] _____ , based on observational data.　5

    The survey covering 138 people, including members of the Seismological Society of Japan, [(2)] _____ .

Natural
22
Slow
24

    Respondents were asked whether a prediction about Nankai mega earthquakes could meet [(3)] _____ : That there is　10 abnormal activity in advance; that the abnormality is observable; that heightening risks could be quickly assessed; and that such an assessment could be announced immediately.

    The questionnaire found that an average of 5.8 percent of their predictions could meet the criteria, while only 19.7 percent of those [(4)] _____　15 _____ about imminent Nankai Trough quakes.

    The massive earthquake off the coast of the Tohoku region in 2011 and other quakes have convinced many experts in Japan that it is impossible to predict earthquakes immediately before they occur.　20

— Based on a report on Kyodo on Japantimes.com —

〈ニュース解説〉　気象庁によると、南海トラフ沿いの大規模地震（マグニチュード８～９クラス）が今後発生する確率は 70 ～ 80 パーセントとされているが、近畿大学が専門家を対象に実施したアンケート調査では南海トラフ地震の予知は 99 パーセント失敗するとの結果が得られ、地震学者達が正確な地震予知を極めて難しいと考えていることが明らかになった。

(Notes)

seismologists 地震学者　**the Pacific off central and western Japan** 東海及び西日本沖合の太平洋［南海トラフ（Nankai Trough）沿いを意味する。南海トラフとは静岡県駿河湾から九州地方沖まで続く水深 4000 メートル級の海底の溝］　**Seismological Society of Japan** 日本地震学会（今回のアンケート調査対象者のほとんどは同学会会員の専門家）　**the massive earthquake off the coast of the Tohoku region in 2011**（2011 年 3 月 11 日に発生した東日本大震災を指す）

■問A (a) ～ (d) のカタカナ語を英語で記せ。

(a) トリアージ

(b) ヘクトパスカル

(c) マグニチュード

(d) ハリケーン

■問B (a) ～ (r) にそれぞれ対応する英語表現を下記の語群から選びその番号を記せ。

(a) （日本の）気象庁　　　　　　(b) 天気予報

(c) 天気図　　　　　　　　　　　(d) 気象衛星

(e) 洪水警報　　　　　　　　　　(f) 津波警報

(g) 雪崩　　　　　　　　　　　　(h) 干ばつ

(i) 寒波　　　　　　　　　　　　(j) 熱波

(k) 余震　　　　　　　　　　　　(l) 火山噴火

(m) 溶岩流　　　　　　　　　　　(n) 地滑り

(o) 低気圧　　　　　　　　　　　(p) 避難所

(q) 救助隊　　　　　　　　　　　(r) 救急車

1. aftershock　　　　　　　　　2. ambulance
3. avalanche　　　　　　　　　4. cold wave
5. drought　　　　　　　　　　6. flood warning
7. heat wave　　　　　　　　　8. Japan Meteorological Agency
9. landslide　　　　　　　　　10. lava flow
11. low pressure (system)　　　12. rescuers
13. shelter　　　　　　　　　　14. tidal wave warning
15. volcanic eruption　　　　　16. weather chart
17. weather forecast　　　　　18. weather satellite

　Chapter 1-10 ではニュースの定義から始めて、ニュースの種類、ニュースの構成要素と組み立て方といったポイントを概観すると共に、紙媒体のニュース、オンラインニュース、映像や音声で伝えるニュースの特質と、これらのニュースの融合化の流れを紹介した。Chapter 11-15 ではジャーナリストがひとつひとつの表現や文章を書く上で留意すべき 5 つの重要点を検討する。

Passive verbs — 受身の動詞

即時性や解り易さを旨とする英文ジャーナリズムの世界では、より直接的で、迫力のある文章を作るため、能動態を用い、動詞の受身用法（be ＋過去分詞）は避けるべき、というのが常識。
　受身用法は、
> 主張内容があいまいになり、文章にインパクトがなくなる
> 主語や主体がわかりにくく、誰の意見か不明で無責任な内容になりやすい
> There is ～や There are ～を使う表現は読者に迂遠で慇懃な感じを与える
> 能動態より be 動詞と動作主を示す by が増えることで文章が長くなる
などのデメリットがある。
パンチのあるニュース記事を書くためには、力強く、直接的でイメージのわく動詞を選ぶ事も大切だ。

このトピックを英文で読んでみよう。

There is a problem many reporters struggle with. The sentences that are written by them are passive. Their phrasing is made awkward because of this, and—wait! *Stop!*

Let's rewrite that paragraph to make it less *passive*:

Many reporters struggle because they write passive sentences. This makes their phrasing awkward.

See the difference? We've strengthened our syntax by starting sentences with their subjects. We've eliminated that clunky phrase *there is*. And we've replaced the verb *to be* (words such as *is* and *are*), with stronger verbs.

You don't have to be a grammar geek to see our point here. Make your sentences *emphatic*. Avoid weak, flabby verbs.

NEWS MEDIA IN THE WORLD

新聞社 Newspapers (2)

✓　米国の新聞は発行部数の少ない地域紙が主流。リベラルな高級紙といわれる *New York Times* や *Washington Post*、*Los Angeles Times* も地方紙だ。米国では、地方紙で研鑽を積んだ記者が高級紙や全国放送の記者に採用されるのが一般的。1980 年代に全米を対象に創刊された *USA Today* も各地域のニュースをフォロー。経済紙の *Wall Street Journal*（略称 WSJ）は、経済通信社の Dow Jones の所有。保守的論調で知られる。

Chapter 12　人口・労働問題

NEWS 12

Disk 2

Japan drifts away from fertility goal as efforts fail to stick

TOKYO ---- Japanese births fell to a new low in 2018 as attempts at work reform designed to accommodate working mothers failed to reverse the trend, highlighting the grave challenge facing one of the world's most rapidly aging countries.

The country had 918,397 births, down by 27,668 from 2017, according to the Ministry of Health, Labor and Welfare. The total fell below 1 million for the third 5 straight year and was roughly a third of the 1949 peak of 2.69 million births.

The fertility rate — the average number of children a woman gives birth to — fell for the third straight year, to 1.42. The government says it wants to increase the figure to 1.8, but has been criticized for not improving conditions that would allow women to balance their careers and child-rearing, despite the rising number of women 10 in the workforce.

"The government deserves some credit for the steps it has taken, such as work-style reforms and making early childhood education and care for young children free," said Masakazu Yamauchi, an associate professor at Waseda University.

Efforts to expand day care capacity have reduced waiting lists in a growing 15 number of cities, including Tokyo. The government has also had some success with measures to reduce long work hours, including a recently imposed cap on overtime with penalties for violation.

But many of its moves focus on those who already have children. Support for young people more generally is limited to things like marriage-oriented matchmaking 20 parties held by local governments.

"It's hard to say that young people's uncertainty about the future has been dispelled," Yamauchi said.

Achieving Japan's desired fertility rate — the average number of children couples wish to have — of 1.8 will require facilitating marriage, birth and child-rearing for all 25 those who want them, regardless of age. This will mean overhauling Japan's traditional system of hiring new graduates right out of school and employing them for life.

Many women worry that taking time off work to have and raise children will harm their prospects of advancement. "I feel like if I get married, there will be restrictions on my time, and I won't be able to move up in my career," said a 28-year- 30 old woman employed at an information technology company.

— Based on a report on Nikkei Asian Review —

〈ニュース解説〉 日本の少子化にストップがかからない。2018 年の合計特殊出生率（1 人の女性が一生涯で生むと推定される子供の数）も 3 年連続で低下し 1.42 となった。政府は様々な対策を導入しているが、十分に奏功していないのが現状。2018 年の出生数も 3 年連続で 100 万人を下回った。出生数の低下が続く原因は、人口の減少と出産年齢の上昇と言われる。日本の第一子の平均出産年齢は 30.7 歳と過去最高を記録している。EU 諸国の中で最も出生率が高いフランスではこの年齢が日本より 2 歳低い 28.7 歳。

(Notes)

◆ (L. 1)　**Japanese births**　日本の出生数

◆ (L. 2)　**accommodate working mothers**　子供を持つ女性が働き続けられるようにする

◆ (L. 5)　**Ministry of Health, Labor and Welfare**　厚生労働省（"Labor" は米国つづり。同省の正式英語名称では英国つづりの "Labour" となっている）

◆ (L. 7)　**fertility rate**　出生率〔正式には "total fertility rate"（合計特殊出生率）〕

◆ (L. 12-13)　**work-style reforms**　働き方改革（働く人々が個々の事情に応じて多様で柔軟な働き方を自分でする選択ことができるようにする改革で、2019 年 4 月から働き方改革法の一部が施行されている）

◆ (L. 14)　**Masakazu Yamauchi, an associate professor at Waseda University**　山内昌和早稲田大学准教授

◆ (L. 17-18)　**cap on overtime with penalties for violation**　（大企業では 2019 年 4 月から、中小企業では 2020 年 4 月から、原則月間 45 時間・年間 360 時間という残業時間の上限が導入され、これに違反すると 6 か月以下の懲役又は 30 万円以下の罰金が課せられることになる）

◆ (L. 20-21)　**marriage-oriented matchmaking parties**　婚活パーティー、お見合いパーティー

◆ (L. 24)　**desired fertility rate**　希望出生率（子供を望む全ての人が希望する人数の子供を産んだ場合の合計特殊出生率。安倍内閣ではアベノミクス「新三本の矢」の中で「夢をつむぐ子育て支援」の目標として 2025 年までに同率を 1.8 まで高めることを目標に掲げている）

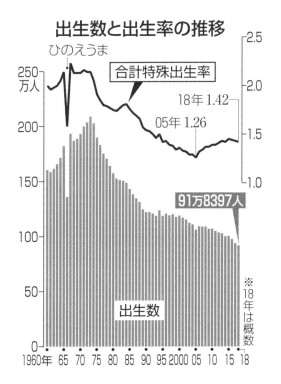

出生数と出生率の推移

ニュースを読んで、下記の設問に答えよ。

1. 本文の内容と一致するものには T (True) を、一致しないものには F (False) を記せ。

(   ) (1) The total number of births in 2018 declined to less than one million for the first time.

(   ) (2) The number of female workers has been declining because of difficulty achieving work-life balance.

(   ) (3) If a company violates the limit on overtime hours, it will be punished.

(   ) (4) Local governments have adopted comprehensive measures to encourage young people to get married.

(   ) (5) Japan is expected to achieve its desired fertility rate easily.

2. 下記は 2019 年 4 月 1 日現在、全国 75 の主要自治体の認可保育施設の待機児童数が 2 年連続で減少し、多大な待機児童の存在という傾向もピークを越えた模様であることを報じた The Mainichi の記事の一部。下記の語群から空所に適語を補充して英文を完成すること。

The number of children waiting to enter (^{1.}   ) day care and other facilities in 75 (^{2.}   ) across Japan stands at 7,894 as of April 2019, down 29 percent from the 2018 figure, Mainichi Shimbun survey has found. The drop in the number marked the second (^{3.}   ) year decline.

The latest survey shows that the (^{4.}   ) of notoriously long waiting lists of children (^{5.}   ) day care spots has apparently (^{6.}   ) its peak nationwide.

— *Based on a report on Mainichi. jp* —

(a)authorized, (b)consecutive, (c)municipalities, (d)passed, (e)seeking, (f)trend

Natural **27**
Slow **29**

TOKYO---The government on Wednesday urged companies to extend employees' retirement to the age of 70 as part of measures to address a severe labor shortage [1] _____.

The government encouraged companies to make efforts to secure employment for workers up to the age of 70 through a host of options such as continued employment after reaching retirement age, [2] _____ _____, financial assistance for freelance contracts, and entrepreneurship support.

Natural **28**
Slow **30**

Many companies set a retirement age of 60, but employees can work until 65 if they desire, and employers are [3] _____.

"It is necessary to provide a variety of options to make use of the expertise of elderly workers," Prime Minister Shinzo Abe said at a gathering to discuss future growth policies. "I want healthy, willing elderly people to [4] _____ _____."

The government [5] _____ next year to revise related laws for stable employment for elderly people, the prime minister said. The government will not make the string of measures mandatory under the revised law, but will consider making it so in the future, sources said.

— *Based on a report on Kyodo on Nikkei Asian Review* —

〈ニュース解説〉　安倍首相を議長とする未来投資会議が発表した 2019 年の成長戦略実行計画案では、さらなる高齢化社会に備えて「全世代型社会保障」を目指した雇用改革が中心に据えられた。今回の改革は、70 歳までの就労確保のための制度として、これまでの定年廃止や定年延長に加えて他企業への転職斡旋、企業支援等を企業側に求めるものとなっている。

(Notes)
entrepreneurship support 起業支援
expertise 専門知識、専門技術
a gathering to discuss future growth policies 未来投資会議（アベノミクスの「三本の矢」の一つである成長戦略を策定するため、首相を議長、関係閣僚や企業代表者等を議員として開催されている会議。英語名称は "Council on Investment for the Future"）

■問A　空所 (a) 〜 (g) にそれぞれ入るべき 1 語を下記の語群から選びその番号を記せ。

合計特殊出生率	→	total (a) rate
幼児死亡率	→	infant (b)
人口密度が高い地域	→	(c) populated area
人口密度が低い地域	→	(d) populated area
人口過密地域	→	(e) area
過疎化地域	→	(f) area
人口動向	→	(g) trend

1. demographic　2. densely　3. depopulated　4. fertility
5. mortality　6. overpopulated　7. sparsely

■問B　(a) 〜 (l) をそれぞれ和訳せよ。

(a) equal employment opportunity

(b) emerging countries

(c) least developed countries

(d) income gap

(e) social security

(f) average life expectancy

(g) minimum wage

(h) ratio of job offers to seekers

(i) pension

(j) health insurance

(k) nursing home

(l) gerontology

Redundancy ― 冗長な文章を避ける

不必要な語や表現を使用すると文章は冗長になる。例えば、形容詞と名詞の組み合わせでは、名詞にその形容詞の意味がもとから含まれている場合にその表現は冗長となる。副詞と動詞の組み合わせにおいても、動詞がその副詞の意味を持つ場合に同様の問題が発生する。ニュースルームでは、記者が作成したニュース原稿は編集デスクに送られ文体や内容のチェックを受けた後、報道される。

このトピックを英文で読んでみよう。

Sometimes it's not so obvious that you're using unnecessary words and phrases. Why say that someone is *currently* president of the club? Or that the game is *scheduled for* Friday night? Or that the victims were burned *in the flames*?

Those italicized words add bulk, but no extra meaning. Just as bad are phrases such as these, which are simply doublespeak:

grateful thanks	true fact	personal opinion
all-time record	end result	serious danger
totally destroyed	very unique	first time ever

Be on the lookout for unnecessary modifiers that *sound* logical but add nothing. Eliminate waste. Edit yourself ruthlessly. As Mark Twain once advised: "When in doubt, strike it out."

新聞社 Newspapers (3)

✓ ロシアのプラウダ（*Pravda*）、中国の人民日報（*People's Daily*）はいずれも両国共産党の機関紙として出発。ソビエト崩壊や中国の近代化により情報発信の多様化が進んだが、報道活動に一定の制限がある中国では政府の意向を窺うメディアとして依然重要。アジアでは、シンガポールの英字紙 *Straits Times* や華字紙の『聯合早報』、タイの英字紙 *Nation*、日本の英字紙 *Japan Times* 等がある。FT や WSJ のアジア版、*New York Times* の世界版である *International New York Times*（かつての *International Herald Tribune*）等が各地で印刷発行されている。

NEWS 13

Disk 2

Amazon to retrain a third of its US workforce

US companies are increasingly paying up to retrain workers as new technologies transform the workplace and companies struggle to recruit talent in one of the hottest job markets in decades.

Amazon.com Inc. is the latest example of a large employer committing to help its workers gain new skills. The online retailer said Thursday it plans to spend $700 ₅ million over about six years to retrain a third of its US workforce as automation, machine learning, and other technology upends the way many of its employees do their jobs.

Companies as varied as AT&T Inc., Walmart Inc., JPMorgan Chase & Co. and Accenture PLC have embarked on efforts to prepare workers for new roles. At a ₁₀ time of historically low unemployment, coupled with rapid digital transformation that requires high-tech job skills, more US companies said they want to help their employees transition to new positions — and they have their bottom line squarely in focus.

"Many have concluded that they must coach existing staff to take on different ₁₅ types of work, or face a dire talent shortage," said Ryan Carson, founder and chief executive of Treehouse, a firm that pairs tech apprentices, often from underrepresented groups, with employers and helps train them.

"It's the beginning of the flood," Mr. Carson said. "We're basically just going back to a time where companies would invest in their own workforces." ₂₀

Though Amazon's training won't carry a stipulation that employees remain with the company, experts say the program is likely to help retain staff. "The ability to hold on to talent is important because recruiting new workers and training them is expensive and time-consuming," said Chris O'Leary, a senior economist at the W.E. Upjohn Institute for Employment Research, a nonprofit research center. "If you can ₂₅ maintain stability, you're lowering your cost," he said.

Amazon's promise to upgrade the skills of its workforce represents one of the biggest corporate retraining initiatives on record and breaks down to about $7,000 per worker, or about $1,200 a year through 2025. By comparison, large employers with 10,000 workers or more that were surveyed by the Association for Talent ₃₀ Development reported spending an average of $500 per worker on training in 2017.

— Based on a report on WSJ.com —

〈ニュース解説〉　アマゾンは米国で従業員数が最も多い企業の一社であり、2019年時点の従業員数は約30万人に上る。しかし、2019年半ば時点で2万のポジション（内半数が本社）が埋められず空席となっている。逼迫する米国の労働市場では求人数が求職者数を上回っており、技能労働者に対する需要は特に高い。

(Notes)

◆ (L. 1)　**pay up**　費用を負担する、支払う
◆ (L. 4)　**Amazon.com, Inc.**　アマゾン・ドット・コム株式会社（米国のECサイト、Webサービス会社。本社：ワシントン州シアトル）
◆ (L. 7)　**machine learning**　機械学習（コンピュータにデータを反復的に学ばせることにより、データに潜む特徴を見つけ出させ、その特徴を新しいデータに適用して分析や予測をする。顔認証や自動運転にもこの技術が利用される）
◆ (L. 9)　**AT&T Inc.**　エイ・ティ・アンド・ティ（米国の情報通信・メディアを傘下に擁する持ち株会社。電話事業では米国最大手。CNNはワーナーメディアの子会社）
◆ (L. 9)　**Walmart Inc.**　ウォルマート（世界最大の米スーパーマーケットチェーン）
◆ (L. 9)　**JPMorgan Chase & Co.**　JPモルガン・チェース（バンク・オブ・アメリカやシティグループと並ぶ米国の巨大銀行持ち株会社）
◆ (L. 10)　**Accenture PLC**　アクセンチュア（アイルランドに登記上の本拠を置く総合コンサルティング会社）
◆ (L. 12)　**high-tech job skills**　ハイテク技能
◆ (L. 13)　**bottom line**　純利益（損益計算書の最終行が純利益であることが語源。売上高は top line と呼ばれることもある。bottom line は、「要点」や「結論」の意味でもしばしば使われる）
◆ (L. 16)　**talent**　才能、技能、才能や技能がある人（々）
◆ (L. 16)　**Ryan Carson**　ライアン・カーソン［米 Treehouse（ツリーハウス）社の創業者兼 CEO（chief executive officer、最高経営責任者）］
◆ (L. 17-18)　**underrepresented group**　マイノリティー・グループ
◆ (L. 21)　**stipulation**　規定、条項
◆ (L. 23)　**hold on to ...**　…を保持する
◆ (L. 24)　**Chris O'Leary**　クリス・オレアリー［W.E. Upjohn Institute for Employment Research（W.E. アップジョン雇用問題研究所）の senior economist（上級エコノミスト）］
◆ (L. 30-31)　**Association for Talent Development**　米 ATD（米国の人材開発協会）

ニュースを読んで、下記の設問に答えよ。

1. 本文の内容と一致するものには T (True) を、一致しないものには F (False) を記せ。

(   ) (1) The US job market is brisk, featuring the abundant and increasing availability of highly skilled workers.

(   ) (2) Many Amazon workers suffer from a mismatch of skills, between those they possess and those required to keep up with ongoing technological advances.

(   ) (3) Like Amazon, major US firms like AT&T are opting to train their existing workers to handle more technologically complex jobs.

(   ) (4) According to Mr. Carson, many companies today think that, without retraining their existing employees, they will face a serious shortage of skilled workers.

(   ) (5) Mr. Carson's comments suggest that the movement among major companies toward retraining their workers is far more than a passing trend.

2. 次の英文を完成させるために、(a) 〜 (d) から最も適切なものを1つ選べ。

(1) Introducing the plan to spend a large amount of money to retrain some of its US workers to acquire high-tech skills, Amazon hopes that_____

   (a) new workers can also be recruited to substitute for existing ones.

   (b) most of the retrained workers will stay with the company.

   (c) the retraining program will help reduce its massive workforce.

   (d) the retraining program will also attract low-skilled workers from abroad.

(2) Amazon's announcement of the retraining program is attracting attention because of _____

   (a) its rivals already adopting programs similar in size.

   (b) the program's focus on both conventional and advanced skills.

   (c) the program's sheer size.

   (d) varied strategies pursued by Amazon and its rivals.

Natural
(33)
Slow
(35)

Scientists are closing in on a long-sought goal — a blood test to screen people for possible signs of Alzheimer's disease and other forms of dementia.

On Monday at the Alzheimer's Association International Conference, half a dozen research groups gave new results on various experimental tests, including one that seems to be [(1)] _____ .　5

Doctors are [(2)] _____ during routine exams, where most dementia symptoms are evaluated, to gauge who needs more extensive testing. Current tools such as brain scans and spinal fluid tests are too expensive or impractical for regular check-ups.

Natural
(34)
Slow
(36)

"We need something quicker and dirtier. [(3)] _____ " to　10 be useful for screening, said Maria Carrillo, the Alzheimer's Association's chief science officer.

Dr. Richard Hodes, director of the National Institute on Aging, called the new results "very promising" and said blood tests soon will be [(4)] _____ _____ for federally funded studies, though it will take a little longer　15 to establish their value in routine medical care.

"In the past year we've [(5)] _____ " on these tests, he said. "This has happened at a pace that is far faster than any of us would have expected."

— Based on a report on VOANews.com —

〈ニュース解説〉　認知症患者は世界で５千万人に昇り、アルツハイマー型が最も多い。現在の医療では認知症の進行を遅らせることは可能だが、根治することは不可能とされている。本ニュースは血液検査により認知症の発症リスクを予測する可能性を示唆している。早期発見により経過観察が可能となるため、治療法の確立につながることが期待されている。

(Notes)
close in on ... …に近づく、迫る　**screen** ふるい掛ける、検査する　**Alzheimer's disease** アルツハイマー病　**dementia** 認知症　**Alzheimer's Association International Conference** アルツハイマー病協会国際会議　**experimental test** 実験的に行われる試験　**routine exam** 定期検査　**extensive testing** 精密検査　**brain scan** 頭部 CT スキャン　**spinal fluid test** 脳脊髄液検査　**quick and dirty** 簡便な　**Maria Carrillo** マリア・カリージョ［Alzheimer's Association（アルツハイマー病協会）の最高科学責任者］　**Richard Hodes** リチャード・ホーズ［National Institute on Aging（米国立老化研究所）の所長］

VOCABULARY BUILDUP

■問A　空所 (a) ～ (f) にそれぞれ入るべき 1 語を下記の語群から選びその番号を記せ。

iPS（人工多能性幹）細胞	→	induced Pluripotent (a) cell
タッチパネル	→	touch (b)
最先端の技術	→	(c)-of-the-art technology
高速増殖炉	→	fast breeder (d)
介護施設	→	nursing-(e) facility
生活習慣病	→	lifestyle-(f) disease

| 1. care | 2. reactor | 3. related |
| 4. screen | 5. state | 6. stem |

■問B　空所 (a) ～ (f) にそれぞれ入るべき 1 語を下記の語群から選びその番号を記せ。

遺伝子組み換え作物	→	genetically (a) crop
太陽光発電	→	(b) power generation
地上波デジタル放送	→	digital (c) broadcasting
医療過誤	→	medical (d)
平均寿命	→	average life (e)
介助犬	→	(f) dog

| 1. error | 2. expectancy | 3. modified |
| 4. service | 5. solar | 6. terrestrial |

■問C　(a) ～ (h) をそれぞれ和訳せよ。

(a) biodegradable plastic
(b) room-temperature superconductivity
(c) shape-memory garments
(d) capsule endoscope
(e) optical fiber
(f) heat stroke
(g) organ transplant
(h) brain death

Long, long, long wordy sentences ― 長い、長い、長い冗漫な文体

小説や論説等でも長くて冗長な文章は敬遠される今日である。ましてや事件や出来事の報道を行うハード・ニュースの記事は正確で簡潔（precise and concise）が生命線。即時報道を目的としないフィーチャー・ニュース、即ち特集記事や読み物においてさえも、長くて取り留めのない文体はニュース記事では避けるべきである。一昔前までは英文で論理を展開する上では理想的な句や節と考えられていた表現方法、或いは過度な丁寧表現のように相手の立場に配慮した言い回しは、ストレートさが欠ける点で逆に文章内容をより複雑にして今日の読者に分かりにくくしている場合もある。ニュース英語のみならずビジネス英語でも同じような状況に遭遇するが、文章は説明口調ではなく簡潔さを保つことによってかえって伝える側の意図が迅速に且つ正確に読者に伝わることはしばしば指摘される。下の英文は、冗漫な文の典型例であるが、冗長な文体を避けるという本課の主旨からすると真逆の書き方でそのような文体を戒めているところが面白い。文章が lengthy 或いは wordy であるということは、退屈な（tedious）文章であることと表裏一体であることを忘れるべきではない。下の英文でも分かるように、文を長くするには様々な表現や方法があるが、文を短く正確に書くことは比較的難しい。

このトピックを英文で読んでみよう。

It should be pointed out that many writers, in order to make themselves sound much more profound and scholarly than perhaps they actually are, use flabby, inflated wording such as "it should be pointed out" and "in order to" and "perhaps"—which we just did ourselves, in fact, earlier in this sentence—in addition to piling up clauses (some using dashes such as those a few words back) or parentheses, such as those in the line above, not to mention semicolons, which often suggest that the writer wants to end the sentence, but just can't bring himself to actually type a period; nonetheless, today's busy readers are too impatient to tolerate the sort of 18th-century pomposity wherein writers, so in love with the sound of their own voices, just go on and on and on and on...

放送 Broadcasting (1)

✓ 20世紀初頭のラジオ、その後のテレビの発達を受け、放送ニュースは即時性と広域性を武器に成長。国際ニュース放送の老舗は英国 BBC（British Broadcasting Corporation）。世界中に広がる取材網を駆使、ラジオの World Service やテレビの BBC World で他をリードしてきた。米国 VOA（Voice of America）は米国国務省の対外宣伝部門として発足。冷戦時代には東側への西側意見の伝達役を担ったが、現在は、世界的なニュース専門機関の地位を確立している。

Chapter 14 スポーツ（1）

NEWS 14
FC Tokyo's Takefusa Kubo seals move to Real Madrid

Disk 2
(37)

Ascendant star playmaker Takefusa Kubo is departing FC Tokyo for a move to Spanish giant Real Madrid, it was announced on Friday. Just days after making his Japan national team debut on Sunday against El Salvador in a pre-Copa America friendly in Rifu, Miyagi Prefecture, the 18-year-old has agreed to terms with Real Madrid with details to be announced in the near future. Real Madrid confirmed the 5 signing in a news release on Friday.

On Thursday, Kubo took part in training with Hajime Moriyasu's squad in San Paulo ahead of the 12-team tournament to be held between Friday and July 7, but left without speaking to reporters. According to Spanish sports newspaper Marca, Kubo has been offered a €1 million salary and a five-year contract, with Real Madrid to 10 pay a €2 million transfer fee to the J. League club. Barcelona and Paris Saint-German were also rumored to be in the running to secure the services of Kubo, who is now free to move after turning 18 on June 4.

(38)

The attacking midfielder has been on a hot scoring streak recently in the J. League first division, netting four goals in his last four games this season. But 15 he now has a chance to make a much bigger splash for one of the world's most prestigious teams.

It will not be Kubo's first taste of Spain, however, as the young prospect was invited to enter the Barcelona youth academy at age 9, earning him the nickname "Japanese Messi." But his first Spanish stint ended in difficult circumstances as, 20 following three seasons in the Barcelona system, he returned to Japan after the club was hit by a transfer ban for breaching FIFA rules on the recruitment of junior players from overseas.

Real Madrid, founded in 1902, has been a powerhouse team for decades. From 1951 to 1960, for example, the team captured five consecutive European Cup titles. 25 Starting in 2016, Real Madrid has won three straight FIFA Club World Cup titles.

— Based on a report on Japantimes.com —

〈ニュース解説〉 FC東京所属の久保建英のレアル・マドリード移籍が決まった。2011年にスペイン・リーグ（リーガ・エスパニョーラ）のFCバルセロナ（通称バルサ）下部組織カンテラ（Cantera）のラ・マシア（La Masia）の入団テストに10歳で合格した久保は、そのままバルサ下部組織でプレイする。しかし、バルサが18歳未満外国人選手の獲得・登録規程に違反したため久保は当地での公式戦出場が認められず、2015年に帰国してFC東京下部組織に入団していた。U-16日本代表としてAFC（アジア・サッカー連盟、Asian Football Confederation）U-16選手権に出場し、FIFA（国際サッカー連盟、フィーファと発音、Fédération Internationale de Football Association）U-17ワールドカップの出場権獲得に貢献。2017年5月にJリーグのトップチームでデビュー。2019年6月までFC東京（途中横浜Fマリノスに期限付き移籍）で活躍していた。レアル・マドリード移籍後、同じくスペインリーグ1部チームのRCDマヨルカに期限付移籍。

(Notes)

◆ **FC Tokyo** FC東京（Jリーグ加盟のプロサッカークラブ。調布市の味の素スタジアムに本拠を置く。過去に長友佑都や中島翔哉等がプレイした）

◆ **Real Madrid** レアル・マドリード［スペインリーグ（リーガ・エスパニョーラ）に加盟しマドリードに本拠を置く世界で最も知られたクラブチームの1つ。かつてクリスティアーノ・ロナウドや現監督のジネディーヌ・ジダン等有名選手がプレイした］

◆ (L. 1) **playmaker** プレイメーカー（試合の流れをコントロールする役割を果たすチームの中心選手で、攻撃的ミッドフィルダー）

◆ (L. 3) **El Salvador** エルサルバドル（中央アメリカ中部に位置する共和国。首都はサンサルバドル）

◆ (L. 3-4) **pre-Copa America friendly** コパ・アメリカ前の親善試合（コパ・アメリカは、南米サッカー連盟が主催するナショナルチームによる大陸選手権。旧称は南米選手権。2019年はブラジルが決勝でペルーを破り優勝。friendlyはfriendly matchのこと）

◆ (L. 4) **Rifu, Miyagi Prefecture** 宮城県利府町［宮城スタジアム（ひとめぼれスタジアム宮城）があり、今回キリンチャレンジカップの日本代表対エルサルバドル戦が開催された。2002年の日韓ワールドカップでは、決勝トーナメント第1戦の日本代表対トルコ代表戦が行われえている］

◆ (L. 7) **Hajime Moriyasu** 森安一（現サッカー日本代表監督。かつて日本代表選手としてもプレイした）

◆ (L. 7-8) **San Paulo** （ブラジルの）サンパウロ市（ブラジルのポルトガル表記ではSão Paulo。人口、経済、文化発信において南米最大の巨大都市。日本人移民の子孫も多く、日本企業が多数進出している。2019年コパ・アメリカの開催地）

◆ (L. 9) **Marca** マルカ紙（スペインのマドリードで発行される日刊スポーツ紙。サッカー関連、特に地元のレアル・マドリードの記事が多い）

◆ (L. 11) **transfer fee** （プロサッカー選手等の）移籍金

◆ (L. 11) **Barcelona** FCバルセロナ（バルセロナのカンプ・ノウをホームスタジアムとするリーガ・エスパニョーラの強豪サッカーチーム。リオネル・メッシやルイス・スアレスのような有名選手が所属する）

◆ (L. 11) **Paris Saint-German** パリ・サンジェルマンFC［パリに本拠を置くフランス・サッカー1部リーグ（リーグ・アン）の強豪チーム。2017年8月にブラジル代表ネイマールが移籍してきたことでも話題となった］

◆ (L. 12) **in the running** 競争に参加して

◆ (L. 14) **attacking midfielder** 攻撃的ミッドフィルダー

◆ (L. 14-15) **J. League first division** Jリーグの1部リーグ（J1リーグのこと）

◆ (L. 19) **Barcelona youth academy** バルセロナ・ユース・アカデミー［FCバルセロナの下部組織（カンテーラと呼ばれる）であるラ・マシアを指す］

◆ (L. 20) **Japanese Messi** 日本のメッシ（世界最高のサッカー選手と評されるFCバルセロナのリオネル・メッシに因んだ呼称）

◆ (L. 21) **Barcelona system** FCバルセロナの組織（実際にはこの組織のなかのバルセロナ・ユース・アカデミーを指す）

◆ (L. 22) **transfer ban** 選手移籍禁止（18歳未満の未成年者保護の観点から、FIFAは移籍条項第19条で未成年者の国際移籍を原則禁止する規程を定めている）

◆ (L. 22) **FIFA** 国際サッカー連盟（フランス語のFédération Internationale de Football Associationの略称。本部はスイスのチューリッヒ）

◆ (L. 25) **European Cup** UEFAチャンピオンズリーグのこと［欧州サッカー連盟（UEFA）主催のクラブチームによるサッカーの大陸選手権。UEFAはUnion of European Football Associationsの略称で、日本語ではウエファ、英語ではユーエイファと発音される］

◆ (L. 26) **FIFA Club World Cup** FIFAクラブ・ワールドカップ（国際サッカー連盟主催のクラブチームによるサッカー世界選手権。2016年以降レアル・マドリードが3連覇中）

1. 本文の内容と一致するものには T (True) を、一致しないものには F (False) を記せ。

(　　) (1) The move by Takefusa Kubo from FC Tokyo to Real Madrid was arranged between the two teams without the knowledge of the Japanese star.

(　　) (2) The transfer of Kubo seems conditional upon his performance during the Copa America.

(　　) (3) There's still a chance the transfer of Kubo may be cancelled when the details of the terms turn out to be disadvantageous for Kubo.

(　　) (4) Twelve teams are involved in the Copa America.

(　　) (5) Losing Kubo from the squad, there's absolutely no merit for FC Tokyo from reaching a transfer agreement with Real Madrid.

(　　) (6) It appears Real Madrid was not the only team that showed interest in Kubo.

(　　) (7) Kubo is old enough to be recruited by European teams without breaching FIFA rules.

(　　) (8) Kubo's first experience in the Spanish football started in Barcelona.

(　　) (9) Kubo had to leave Spain under Real Madrid's legal complication with the FIFA regarding the contracts with overseas underage players.

(　　) (10) Real Madrid has been one of the most prestigious football teams not just in Spain but also throughout the world.

2. 次の説明に相当するサッカー用語を下の語群から選び、その語を空所に入れよ。

(1) a player who protects the goal by stopping any penetration of the ball into the goal (　　　　　　)

(2) using one's head to move a football in the air to score a goal (　　　　　　)

(3) a place kick awarded, either direct or indirect, due to a penalty by the other team outside the penalty area (　　　　　　)

(4) a player, usually an offensive midfielder, who is particularly good at controlling the flow of the team's offensive play (　　　　　　)

[free kick,　goalie,　header,　midfielder,　penalty kick,　playmaker,　sideback]

音声を聞き、下線部を補え。（２回録音されています。１回目はナチュラルスピード、２回目はスロースピードです。）

Natural (39)
Slow (41)

Washington Wizards fans can expect to see Rui Hachimura "play hard" every time he takes the floor, the NBA team's first-round draft pick said Friday.

Fronting the media [(1)] _____ at Washington's Capital One Arena, the NBA's ninth overall pick said he would continue playing the high-energy brand of basketball that [(2)] _____ as a forward   5
for Gonzaga University.

"I come out with good energy. Offensively, defensively…I'm just going to play hard, every game," said Hachimura, a day after [(3)] _____ taken in the opening round of the NBA draft.

Natural (40)
Slow (42)

Dressed sharply in a black checked suit, black shirt and maroon tie,   10
Hachimura [(4)] _____ alongside Wizards coach Scott Brooks and interim general manager Tommy Sheppard, smiling and cracking jokes during the conference.

Answering questions from reporters in English, [(5)] _____
_____ he barely spoke upon arriving at Gonzaga, a college located   15
in Spokane, Washington State, in 2016.

While some rookies might be overwhelmed by the media attention, the crowd of journalists at the Wizards' headquarters was a familiar sight for Hachimura, already the biggest basketball star his country has ever produced.

— *Based on a report on Japantimes. com* —

〈ニュース解説〉　ベナン人の父と日本人の母を持つ富山県出身の八村塁は、宮城県の高校卒業後アメリカのゴンザガ大学に進み、同大学バスケットボール部で活躍。2019 年 NBA（全米プロバスケットボール協会）ドラフトでは、ワシントン・ウィザーズから一巡目９位指名を受ける。

(Notes)
Washington Wizards ワシントン・ウィザーズ［ワシントン D.C. に本拠を置く NBA のチーム。かつては「ブレッツ」（Bullets）のチーム名であったが銃規制の社会的風潮もあり、Wizards（魔法使い）に名称変更。以前マイケル・ジョーダンもプレイした］　**Rui Hachimura** 八村塁　**Capital One Arena** キャピタル・ワン・アリーナ［ワシントン D.C. にある屋内競技場。ウィザーズの他にナショナル・ホッケー・リーグ（NHL）のワシントン・キャピタルズの本拠も置かれる］　**Gonzaga University** ゴンザガ大学［アメリカ・ワシントン州のスポケーンにある私立大学でバスケットボールの名門校。ゴンザガは、16 世紀イタリアのイエズス会士アロイシウス・ゴンザーガ（Aloysius Gonzaga）に由来］　**Scott Brooks** スコット・ブルックス（元 NBA プレーヤー。ポイントガードとして各チームを渡り歩く。現在ワシントン・ウィザーズのヘッドコーチを務める）　**Tommy Sheppard** トミー・シェパード（現在ワシントン・ウィザーズの暫定統括マネージャー）

VOCABULARY BUILDUP

■問A 相撲で用いられる次の用語に対する英語表現を下記の語群から選びその番号を記せ。

(a) 寄り切り　　　　(b) つり出し　　　　(c) 上手投げ

(d) 下手投げ　　　　(e) まげ　　　　　　(f) 親方

(g) 押し出し　　　　(h) 土俵入り　　　　(i) 横綱

> 1. forcing out　　　2. grand champion　　　3. lifting out
> 4. overarm throw　　5. pushing out　　　　6. ring entering ceremony
> 7. stable master　　8. topknot　　　　　　9. underarm throw

■問B (a) ～ (g) の体操用語にそれぞれ対応する日本語表現を下記の語群から選びその番号を記せ。

(a) balance beam　(b) floor exercises　(c) flying rings　(d) horse vault

(e) parallel bars　(f) pommel horse　(g) uneven bars

> 1. あん馬　　　2. 段違い平行棒　　　3. 跳馬　　　4. つり輪
> 5. 平均台　　　6. 平行棒　　　　　　7. ゆか

■問C 下記のそれぞれの語群の中から正しいものを選びその番号を記せ。

【サッカー用語】

a. ロスタイム	→	1. injury time	2. loss time
b. シュート	→	1. shoot	2. shot
c. オウンゴール	→	1. own goal	2. aun goal

【ゴルフ用語】

d. ティーオフ	→	1. tea-off	2. tee-off
e. ボギー	→	1. bogey	2. bogy
f. パー	→	1. par	2. per
g. バーディー	→	1. bardie	2. birdic

【野球用語】

h. コールドゲーム	→	1. called game	2. cold game
i. スクイズ	→	1. squeeze bunt	2. squiz bunt
j. ライナー	→	1. line drive	2. rhine drive
k. ゴロ	→	1. go-low	2. grounder
l. フライ	→	1. fly	2. fry
m. フォアボール	→	1. base on balls	2. four balls
n. サウスポー	→	1. southpaw	2. southpour
o. ホームラン	→	1. homerun	2. home run

Jargon and journalese ― 専門用語とジャーナリズム調の文体

ニュースにとって最も重要なことは「分かりやすい」ことだ。誰もが忙しい現代、基本的に「読み捨て」される新聞記事は誰が読んでもきちんと内容が伝わること、いちいち読み返さなくても分かることが非常に重要だからである。英語の新聞の場合でも、難解な言葉や表現を避け、単語そのものもできるだけわかりやすい short words を用いる。例えば purchase → buy、attempt → try、anticipate → expect、utilize → use、request → ask、obtain → get などである。しかし、時に新聞記事は陳腐で大げさなジャーナリズム的表現に陥りがちであることも事実だ。

このトピックを英文で読んでみよう。

Bureaucrats love to use words like *utilize*, *finalize* and *structured*. Cops like to say suspects are *apprehended* and *incarcerated*. And if you're a campus spokesman, why would you want to say "*the school can't afford to pay raises*" when you could say "*the salary scale revision will adversely affect the university's financial stability*"?

Good reporters relentlessly strive to filter out bloated, convoluted jargon and officialese. And those who don't should be *redirected*, *transitioned* or *subject to personnel surplus reduction* (i.e., fired).

But reporters often lapse into "journalese" without realizing it. Journalese, as veteran editor Joe Grimm puts it, is the peculiar language that newspapers have evolved that reads like this:

Negotiators yesterday, in an eleventh-hour decision following marathon talks, hammered out an agreement on a key wage provision they earlier had rejected.

That's not as bad as bureaucratic gobbledygook. But it's still a problem, because it's still full of clichés.

NEWS MEDIA IN THE WORLD

放送 Broadcasting (2)

✓ 放送産業の故郷米国では、ラジオ放送についで、1940 年代には商業テレビ放送が開始。CBS（Columbia Broadcasting System）、NBC（National Broadcasting Company）、ABC（American Broadcasting Company）の 3 大ネットワーク時代が続いたが、現在では FOX を含め 4 大ネットワークと呼ばれることもある。さらに地上波放送に飽き足らない視聴者のニーズに応える形でケーブルテレビが急拡大。80 年代には CNN（Cable News Network）が衛星放送による世界初のニュース専門テレビ局として誕生。衛星放送が東側住民へ情報を提供し、冷戦終結に貢献したという評価もある。

NEWS 15

Disk 2
(43)

Japan making the top eight at 2019 Rugby World Cup will be no easy task

Japan coach Jamie Joseph said earlier this week that his team's "Rugby World Cup final goal would be making the top eight." But for a side hoping to get to the quarterfinals next year in Japan, a 3-4 record for 2018 is, at first glance, hardly the ideal preparation. After all, as the Brave Blossoms know only too well from 2015, even winning three out of four games in a World Cup pool doesn't guarantee a spot in ₅ the last eight.

Back in May 2017, when the draw was made, many Japanese thought Japan had got it easy after it had been paired up with Ireland, Scotland, the playoff winner (Samoa) and the top European qualifier, which eventually proved to be Russia. But, in Pool A where Japan will play in the group stage, Ireland is arguably the No. 1 team ₁₀ in the world right now, Scotland is forever improving, Russia showed it will be a massive physical threat, while any team that writes off Samoa does so at its own peril.

But before anyone labels me a doom merchant, it is important to recall that just two tournaments ago, the Brave Blossoms' ambitions were considerably lower than now. John Kirwan's team went to New Zealand hoping to pick up two wins. It came ₁₅ back with just a draw with Canada.

The lack of self-belief was a common trait throughout Japanese rugby, and it was even more of a problem at international level as the old excuse of "Japan not being big enough" kept getting used. Perhaps the biggest legacy of Eddie Jones' tenure was the mental toughness that the Brave Blossoms developed whereby they never gave ₂₀ up hope they could win a game — the most obvious example being those last few minutes against South Africa in Brighton three years ago.

While Joseph is still talking about size being a problem, the mental side of things has continued to develop and was very much evident in the autumn, following games in June that saw them split a two-game series with Italy and beat Georgia. A poor first ₂₅ half against the World XV at the end of October in Osaka was followed by a spirited comeback. "We could have drawn the game, but our mindset was to win as only a win will get you into the last eight at the World Cup," Joseph said of their 31-28 defeat.

So which Japan will turn up next year? The Brave Blossoms, by their coach's own admission, still don't have 30 players that are good enough to play test-match ₃₀ rugby. "One of our biggest challenges has always been depth," Joseph said. "If a Tier 1 country gets a few injuries, they can replace them with players just as good. That's not the case with Japan."

— Based on a report on Japantimes. com —

〈ニュース解説〉 2019年のラグビー・ワールドカップは、9月20日から11月2日まで日本で開催。目標は一次リーグで属するプールAを勝ち抜き、ベスト8となって決勝トーナメントに進むことである。しかし、同プールではアイルランドやスコットランド等強豪と戦わねばならず、一次リーグ突破は容易ではない。英文では、2019年ワールドカップ日本大会のみならず、2015年のロンドン大会、2011年のニュージーランド大会への言及がある。

(Notes)

◆ **2019 Rugby World Cup** 2019ラグビー・ワールドカップ［2019年開催のラグビー・ワールドカップ日本大会（Rugby World Cup 2019、RWC2019と略記）を指す。ワールドカップは4年に1度のラグビー界最大の国際大会］

◆ (L. 1) **Jamie Joseph** ジェイミー・ジョセフ（イングランド代表ヘッドコーチに転出したエディー・ジョーンズに代わって2016年より日本代表ヘッドコーチに就任。元ニュージーランド代表プレーヤー。ヘッドコーチは、野球では監督の下の役職であるが、ラグビーでは監督を指す）

◆ (L. 3) **quarterfinals** 準々決勝（ラグビー・ワールドカップでは、一次リーグの各プール上位2チームがベスト8となって準々決勝に進出する。準決勝はsemifinals）

◆ (L. 4) **Brave Blossoms** ブレイブ・ブロッサムズ［ラグビー日本代表の愛称。代表のユニフォームに付けられた桜（チェリー・ブロッサム）のエンブレムにちなむ］

◆ (L. 4) **from 2015** 2015年（の経験）から［2015年にイングランド（一部ウェールズ）で開催された第8回ラグビー・ワールドカップで、日本代表は3勝を挙げながら決勝トーナメント進出を逸したことを指す。ニュージーランドが2大会連続3度目の優勝に輝き、日本も決勝トーナメントへの進出は逃したものの、予選プールでは強豪南アフリカを破っている］

◆ (L. 8) **the playoff winner（Samoa）** プレーオフ勝者サモア（2015年のワールドカップで日本を含め各プールで上位3位以上の国は、自動的にRWC2019に出場。その後、ヨーロッパ、オセアニア、アメリカ、アフリカでそれぞれ地区予選があり、ジョージア、フィジー、トンガ、アメリカ合衆国、ナミビアが出場権を獲得。さらに、ヨーロッパ・オセアニア・プレーオフ予選で、サモアがドイツを破りプレーオフ勝者としてRWC2019への出場権を獲得）

◆ (L. 10) **Pool A** プールA（RWC2019では、出場国は予選プールABCDの4つのプールに振り分けられ、各プールでは5か国が決勝トーナメントに向けてプール内上位2か国に入るべく熱戦が繰り広げられる。日本はプールAに入る）

◆ (L. 13) **doom merchant** 悲観論者（doomsayerとも言う）

◆ (L. 14) **two tournaments ago** 2大会前［RWC2019の2大会前の第7回ワールドカップ（RWC2011）を指す。ニュージーランドで開催され、開催国が優勝］

◆ (L. 15) **John Kirwan's team** ジョン・カーワンのチーム（即ち日本代表。カーワンは2007年から2011年のRWC2011ニュージーランド大会まで日本代表ヘッドコーチを務める。RWC2011では、日本は4戦1分3敗で一時予選敗退）

◆ (L. 19) **Eddie Jones** エディー・ジョーンズ（現イングランド代表ヘッドコーチ。2012年から2015年まで日本代表のヘッドコーチを務め、RWC2015予選プールでの南アフリカに対する歴史的勝利を導いた）

◆ (L. 22) **Brighton** ブライトン（イングランド南東部に位置する海浜リゾート市。語学学校も多い）

◆ (L. 26) **The World XV** 世界選抜チーム（2018年10月に東大阪市の花園ラグビー場で行われたジャパン・ラグビー・チャレンジマッチ2018に出場。世界選抜チームは、ラグビー強豪国を中心に有力選手を集め、非公式且つ特別に編成されるチームで、重要な試合ではあるが、一般に後掲のテストマッチとは区別される）

◆ (L. 30) **test-match rugby** ラグビー・テストマッチ（テストマッチとは、国と国との誇りをかけた代表チーム同士の国際試合。テストマッチという言葉は、主にラグビーやクリケットで使われる）

◆ (L. 31-32) **Tier 1 country** ティア1の国［ティア1（Tier one）とは、ラグビー・チャンピオンシップに参戦する南半球4か国（ニュージーランド、オーストラリア、南アフリカ、アルゼンチン）とシックス・ネイションズ・チャンピオンシップを戦う欧州6か国（イングランド、フランス、アイルランド、スコットランド、ウェールズ、イタリア）の合計10か国から構成されるラグビー強豪国を指す。最近イタリアの世界ランクは落ちているが、ティア1の国々はワールドカップでの試合日程等でも優遇を受ける。日本はティア2］

ニュースを読んで、下記の設問に答えよ。

1. 本文の内容と一致するものには T (True) を、一致しないものには F (False) を記せ。

(   ) (1) As Japan is the host nation for the 2019 Rugby World Cup (RWC), the advancement of the Brave Blossoms to the quarterfinals is guaranteed.

(   ) (2) Japan's record in 2018 was good enough to create high expectations among Japanese fans for the 2019 RWC.

(   ) (3) Even with three wins in the group stage of the 2015 RWC, Japan failed to reach the quarterfinals.

(   ) (4) Japan's initial response following the draw for the group stage for the 2019 RWC was rather optimistic.

(   ) (5) In Pool A of the group stage, winning the matches against Russia and Samoa will be no easy task.

(   ) (6) At the 2011 RWC in New Zealand, Japan was aiming to win two games, but failed to win any.

(   ) (7) One of Eddie Jones' contributions to the Brave Blossoms was that he helped Japanese rugby players enhance their mental toughness.

(   ) (8) According to Jamie Joseph, the old excuse of "Japan not being big enough" does not reflect the size and sturdiness of the present Japanese squad.

(   ) (9) Jamie Joseph failed to maintain the tradition initiated by Eddie Jones to strengthen the mental side of the players.

(   ) (10) Despite a less than ideal first half during the match against the World XV, Japan eventually managed to win the game.

(   ) (11) Jamie Joseph believes that one of the weaknesses of the Brave Blossoms lies in its lack of a large pool of good reserve players.

2. (a) ～ (f) のラグビー用語の英文の説明に対応する英語を下記の語群から選びその番号を記せ。

(a) The eight forwards from each team binding together and pushing against each other (   )

(b) The area where a player must remain for a minimum of 10 minutes after being shown a yellow card (   )

(c) An offence whereby a player deliberately impedes an opponent who does not have the ball (   )

(d) A charge executed on a player who has already passed or kicked away the ball (   )

(e) A physical contact that is formed, usually following a tackle, when the ball is on the ground and players from two opposing teams meet over the ball (   )

(f) The player who usually wears jersey number 15 and acts as the last line of defence (   )

1. fullback   2. late tackle   3. obstruction   4. ruck   5. scrum   6. sin bin

EXERCISE 2

音声を聞き、下線部を補え。（２回録音されています。１回目はナチュラルスピード、２回目はスロースピードです。）

Natural 45
Slow 47

The same night the Toronto Raptors won Canada's first NBA championship, baseball phenom Shohei Ohtani [(1)] _____. The Los Angeles Angels' designated hitter batted a single, double, triple and home run all in the same game — what's known in the sport as a "cycle" — and became [(2)]

_____.

Ohtani, 24, started backwards with a home run in the first inning, then a double in the third and a triple in the fifth in the away game versus the Tampa Bay Rays. He clinched it in the top of the seventh inning with a single to right-center field. The Angels won the game 5-3, [(3)] _____.

Natural 46
Slow 48

It was a thrilling moment in a stale season for the Angels, [(4)] _____ _____ of the American League West standings with 34 wins and 35 losses.

Since his 2018 debut, Ohtani's been hailed as the "Japanese Babe Ruth" for his winning starts as both a pitcher and designated hitter, a rarity in Major League Baseball. But after an elbow injury and the Tommy John surgery that followed delayed his pitching start to 2020, he's stuck strictly to batting — and consistently delivers.

Center fielder Mike Trout was the last Angel [(5)] _____, the team said.

— Based on a report on CNN.com —

〈ニュース解説〉　日本球界からメジャーリーグ（英語の発音はメイジャーリーグ）のロサンゼルス・エンゼルスに移籍した大谷翔平は、2018 年シーズンでは投手と打者の両方で活躍し、アメリカンリーグの新人王に選ばれた。シーズン終了後トミー・ジョン手術（靭帯再建手術）を受けた大谷は、手術後のリハビリの影響で投手としての起用は 2019 年シーズン中はないと言われる中、シーズン途中の 5 月 7 日から打者として試合出場を果たし、6 月 13 日には日本人メジャーリーガー初のサイクルヒットを達成した。メジャーリーグは合計 30 球団から成る世界最高峰のプロ野球リーグ。メジャーリーグの別称が Big League であることから「大リーグ」とも呼ばれる。ナショナルリーグとアメリカンリーグの 2 リーグから成り、それぞれ東地区、中地区、西地区に分けられる。

(Notes)

Tronto Raptors トロント・ラプターズ［カナダのトロントに本拠を置く NBA（National Basketball Association、北米で展開する世界最高峰の男子プロバスケットボールリーグ）イースタン・カンファレンスのチーム。NBA の 30 チーム中、アメリカ合衆国に本拠地を置かない唯一のチーム。2018-19 年シーズンで初優勝に輝く］　**baseball phenom Shohei Ohtani** 野球界の天才大谷翔平（phenom は Phenomenon の短縮形）　**designated hitter** 指名打者（DH と略記）　**cycle** サイクルヒット［１つの試合で一人の打者が単打（single）、二塁打（double）、三塁打（triple）、本塁打（home run）をそれぞれ 1 本以上打つこと］　**Tampa Bay Rays** タンパベイ・レイズ（メジャーリーグのアメリカンリーグ東地区のチーム。フロリダ州セントピーターズバーグが本拠地。2007 年にリーグ優勝するもワールドシリーズで敗退）　**clinch** 片をつける　**the top of the seventh inning** 7 回表（裏は bottom を使う）　**American League West** アメリカンリーグ西地区　**Japanese Babe Ruth** 日本のベーブ・ルース（大打者ベーブ・ルースも当初投手と打者の二刀流であったことから）　**winning starts** 見事なスタート（2018 年にメジャーリーグ移籍を果たした大谷が、投手と指名打者の二刀流として見事なスタートを切ったことを指す。肘の故障を訴えてからは、残りのシーズンは打者に専念）　**Tommy John Surgery** トミー・ジョン手術（フランク・ジョーブが考案した靭帯再建手術。投手であったトミー・ジョンが初めてこの手術を受けたことに因む呼称）　**deliver**（安打を）打つ　**Mike Trout** マイク・トラウト（ロサンゼルス・エンゼルスに属するメジャーリーグを代表する打者）

■問A (a) 〜 (i) にそれぞれ対応する英語表現を下記の語群から選びその番号を記せ。

(a) 円盤投げ   (b) 砲丸投げ   (c) やり投げ

(d) ハンマー投げ   (e) 走高跳び   (f) 走幅跳び

(g) 三段跳び   (h) 棒高跳び   (i) 十種競技

1. decathlon	2. discus throw	3. hammer throw
4. high jump	5. javelin throw	6. long jump
7. pole vault	8. shot put	9. triple jump

■問B (a) 〜 (h) の野球用語の説明に対応する英語を下記の語群から選びその番号を記せ。

(a) The extension of a baseball game until one team is ahead of the other at the end of an inning

(b) An out resulting from a batter getting three strikes during a time at bat

(c) Getting two players out on one play

(d) An act of deliberately hitting a baseball gently without swinging the bat so that it does not roll far into the infield

(e) A pitch that the catcher should have caught but missed, allowing runners to advance to the next base

(f) A relief pitcher who specializes in protecting a lead by getting the final outs in a close game

(g) A way of measuring a pitcher's effectiveness

(h) A pitch of a baseball that does not travel straight, as it is thrown with spin so that its path curves as it approaches the batter

1. breaking ball	2. bunt	3. closer	4. double play
5. earned run average	6. extra innings	7. passed ball	8. strikeout

■問C フィギュアスケートのトリプルジャンプで、浅田真央選手が跳んだ3回転半のジャンプの名称を、下記の語群から選びその番号を記せ。

1. triple axel	2. triple loop	3. triple lutz	4. triple salchow

Clichés（クリシェ）— 使い古された常套句

クリシェ（cliché）はフランス語語源で、「使い古され手垢がついてしまった陳腐な常套句」を意味する。元々は目新しくインパクトのある表現だったが、あまりにも使われすぎたため陳腐化してしまった比喩、イディオム、キャッチフレーズ、（聖書、文学作品、映画のセリフ等からの）引用、ことわざ、外来語、流行語などが含まれる。ライターの頭の中にはクリシェが定着してしまっているので、ニュースを書く際にも安易に、あるいは、無意識にクリシェを使ってしまいがちである。しかし、クリシェの使用は文を空疎で魅力のないものにしてしまう危険性があるので、できるだけ回避するのが望ましいとされている。*The New York Times Manual of Style and Usage* でも、「クリシェを用いる場合にはそれらを用いることに妥当性があるか否か（whether their use can be justified）を慎重に検討すべきだが、大抵の場合、その使用に妥当性はない」としている。クリシェと思われる表現をニュースの中で使おうとする場合には、その適切性・新鮮味をきちんと吟味することが必須である。*News Reporting and Writing*（Menche, 1987）によると、英国の作家でジャーナリストでもある George Orwell（ジョージ・オウェル）も、「印刷物で見慣れた表現を使用する時には常に慎重に」とライターに警告している。

このトピックを英文で読んでみよう。

Beyond the shadow of a doubt, you should work 24/7 to avoid clichés like the plague. Hel-*lo*? It's a no-brainer. Go ahead—make my day.

Tired, worn-out clichés instantly lower the IQ of your writing. So do corny newswriting clichés (a form of journalese) like these:

The *close-knit community* was *shaken by the tragedy*.

Tempers flared over a laundry list of complaints.

The *embattled mayor* is *cautiously optimistic*, but *troubled youths* face an *uncertain future* sparked by *massive blasts* in *bullet-riddled, shark-infested waters*.

So *now begins the heartbreaking task of cleaning up*.

Yes, clichés *can* come in handy. And yes, a skilled writer can use them in clever ways. Once in a blue moon.

NEWS MEDIA IN THE WORLD

放送 Broadcasting (3)

✓ CNN の成功を受け、90 年代以降ニュース専門チャンネルが続々登場。米国では、映像産業から派生した米国 FOX ニュースが参入。中東カタールにはアル・ジャジーラ（Al Jazeera）が誕生。インターネットとの融合による映像情報サービスの拡大を背景に、既存ニュース・メディアも含めた世界大のメディアミックス競争が進行中だ。

参考文献

R.E. Garst & T.M. Bernstein, *Headlines and Deadlines*, Columbia University Press (1963)

L.A. Campbell & R.E. Wolseley, *How to Report and Write the News*, Prentice-Hall (1961)

Tim Harrower, *Inside Reporting*, McGraw-Hill (2009)

The Missouri Group, *News Reporting and Writing*, Bedford / St Martins (2010)

William E. Blundell, *The Art and Craft of Feature Writing based on The Wall Street Journal Guide*, Plume (1988)

Darrell Christian, *The Associated Press Stylebook 2010 and Briefing on Media Law*, Associated Press (2010)

Rene J. Cappon, *The Associated Press Guide to News Writing*, 3rd ed., ARCO (2005),

Bill Kovach & Tom Rosenstiel, *The Elements of Journalism*, Three Rivers Press (2007)

Allan M. Siegal and William G. Connolly, *The New York Times Manual of Style and Usage*, Three Rivers Press (1999)

Paul R. Martin, (2002), *The Wall Street Journal Essential Guide to Business Style and Usage*, Free Press (2002)

Thomas W. Lippman, *The Washington Post Desk-Book on Style*, 2nd ed., McGraw-Hill (1989)

Brian S. Brooks & James L. Pinson, *Working with Words*, 2nd ed., St. Martin,s Press (1993)

Carole Rich, *Writing and Reporting News*, 5th ed., Thomson Wadsworth (2002)

藤井章雄，『放送ニュース英語　音を読む』，朝日出版社（1983）

藤井章雄，『ニュース英語がわかる本』，PHP 研究所（1992）

藤井章雄，『ニュース英語の翻訳プロセス』，早稲田大学出版部（1996）

藤井章雄，『放送ニュース英語の体系』，早稲田大学出版部（2004）

日本英語コミュニケーション学会紀要　第 7 巻（1998），8 巻（1999），11 巻（2002），12 巻（2003），13 巻（2004），15 巻（2006），17 巻（2008），18 巻（2009），19 巻（2010），20 巻（2011），21 巻（2012），22 巻（2013）

時事英語の総合演習
— 2020 年度版 —

検印 省略	ⓒ 2020年 1 月31日　第 1 版発行

編著者	堀江　　洋文
	加藤　　香織
	小西　　和久
	宮崎　　修二
	内野　　泰子
発行者	原　　　雅久
発行所	株式会社　朝 日 出 版 社

101-0065　東京都千代田区西神田 3-3-5
電話　東京 (03)3239-0271
FAX　東京 (03)3239-0479
e-mail　text-e@asahipress.com
振替口座　00140-2-46008
組版／製版・信毎書籍印刷株式会社